# SAYINGS OF J. KRISHNAMURTI

# Sayings of J. Krishnamurti

COMPILED BY
SUSUNAGA WEERAPERUMA

MOTILAL BANARSIDASS PUBLISHERS
PRIVATE LIMITED • DELHI

*First Edition: Bombay, 1986*
*Second Edition: Bombay, 1989*
*Third Edition: Delhi, 1996*



ISBN: 81-208-1421-5



*Also available at:*

**MOTILAL BANARSIDASS**
41 U.A. Bungalow Road, Jawahar Nagar, Delhi 110 007
8 Mahalaxmi Chamber, Warden Road, Mumbai 400 026
120 Royapettah High Road, Mylapore, Madras 600 004
Sanas Plaza, Subhash Nagar, Pune 411 002
16 St. Mark's Road, Bangalore 560 001
8 Camac Street, Calcutta 700 017
Ashok Rajpath, Patna 800 004
Chowk, Varanasi 221 001

PRINTED IN INDIA
BY JAINENDRA PRAKASH JAIN AT SHRI JAINENDRA PRESS,
A-45 NARAINA, PHASE I, NEW DELHI 110 028
AND PUBLISHED BY NARENDRA PRAKASH JAIN FOR
MOTILAL BANARSIDASS PUBLISHERS PRIVATE LIMITED,
BUNGALOW ROAD, DELHI 110 007

Dedicated to

# KRISHNAJI

This compilation is dedicated to our beloved Krishnaji who passed away on 17th February 1986 at Pine Cottage, Ojai, California.

His physical presence is no more but his immortal teachings will be cherished for all time.

Thy life is a death;
Death is a rebirth.
Happy is the man
That is beyond the clutches
Of their limitations.

—Krishnamurti

*The Song of life*

# PREFACE

In May 1985 Sri J. Krishnamurti very kindly invited me for lunch at Arya Vihar, his home in Ojai, California. This was a memorable occasion as it occurred only a few days after his 90th birthday. After a delicious vegetarian meal I informed Krishnaji that I was planning to compile for publication an anthology of quotations from his writings. He then inquired whether this book was going to be like *The Perennial Philosophy* by his late friend, Aldous Huxley. I replied that it would be similar to Huxley's compilation in some respects but I would be selecting shorter passages and pithy sentences for inclusion. Then our discussion turned to the problem of finding a suitable title for the book. I suggested the title 'The Wisdom of Krishnamurti'. Krishnaji said: "That's too grand! Why not call it *Sayings of Krishnamurti?*". That he preferred a simple title to a grand one is so typical of his modest and self-effacing character.

This book is nothing more than a collection of his sayings up to the year 1968.

Like a beautiful garland of many fragrant flowers, these selections have been taken from his utterances on a wide range of spiritual and philosophical subjects. I have painstakingly tried to present in this volume the quintessence of the message of one of the greatest teachers of all time.

At the end of every quotation is a statement indicating its source. In this way the interested reader is helped not only to check the authenticity of a quotation but also its context.

It is hoped that those who come upon this volume

would be stimulated to read and study Krishnamurti's own works of which fortunately there are a great many in existence. Those who discover his books will find that they open a door to a new world, a new approach to life and a heightened sensitivity.

I have carefully avoided the inclusion of quotations from the pre-1927 period because these are not always representative of Krishnamurti's present teachings. To illustrate this point it is necessary to quote a few lines from one of my own books, *Supplement to A Bibliography of the Life and Teachings of Jiddu Krishnamurti* (Bombay: Chetana, 1982) p.xii-xiii:

> 'By breaking through the shell of the self, the restrictive psychological "I", Krishnamurti had at last found that freedom which has been the spiritual quest of man throughout the ages. In an address delivered at Eerde on *August 2nd, 1927*, he said: "I could not have said last year, as I can say now, that I am the Teacher; for had I said it then it would have been insincere, it would have been untrue ...But now I can say it. I have become one with the Beloved. I have been made simple. I have become glorified because of Him, and because of Him I can help. My purpose is not to create discussions on authority, on manifestations in the personality of Krishnamurti, but to give the waters that shall wash away your sorrows, your petty tyrannies, your limitations, so that you will be free, so that you will eventually join that ocean where there is no limitation, where there is the Beloved." This date needs remembering because it marks an important turning point in his life. *The publications of Krishnamurti, in a sense, conveniently fall into two categories: first, those belonging to the years of his preparation and search; second, those since his spiritual illumination.*'

November, 1985 Susunaga Weeraperuma

## ACKNOWLEDGEMENTS

I am very grateful to Mr. D. Rajagopal and the K & R Foundation for granting permission to quote from J. Krishnamurti's books that belong to the pre-1968 period.

Apart from the other remarkable books that were produced by him, in 1954 Mr. Rajagopal rendered a great service by having been responsible for *The First and Last Freedom*. People in different parts of the world were introduced to the teaching via this fine work. I am confident that *Sayings of J. Krishnamurti* will help further in the wider dissemination of the teaching.

I am particularly thankful to Sri Sudhakar S. Dikshit of Chetana for asking me to compile this work. His proposal was wholeheartedly accepted and implemented, especially because ever since the 1950s Chetana has done so much to spread the message of Krishnaji through their various publications.

November, 1985

# CONTENTS

Appendix

# Action

1

When you question and analyze action, you put an end to action. But if you are aware, if you are intense in your action, if you give to it your whole mind and heart, then that action will reveal whether you are thereby seeking comfort, security, or that infinite understanding which is the eternal movement of life.

*Verbatim Reports of Talks and Answers . . .Adyar, India 1933-34 p.35*

2

You cannot understand after action has taken place, which would be self-analysis, but only in the moment of action itself. You can be fully aware only in action.

*Verbatim Reports of Talks and Answers . . Adyar, India 1933-34 p.84*

3

There cannot be a world transformation, a revolution, as long as action is based on ideas; because action then is merely reaction; therefore ideas become much more important than action, and that is precisely what is taking place in the world, isn't it? To act, we must discover the impediments that prevent action. But most of us don't want to act — that is our difficulty. We prefer to discuss, we prefer to substitute one ideology for another, and so we escape from action through ideology.

*Krishnamurti's Talks 1949-1950 (Verbatim Report) ... Ceylon p.10*

4

It is only when the mind is free of idea and belief that it can act rightly.

*Krishnamurti's Talks 1949-1950 (Verbatim Report) ... Ceylon p.10*

5

As long as action is the outcome of the past, action can never be free; and only in freedom can you discover what is true. What happens is that, as the mind is not free, it cannot act; it can only react; and reaction is the basis of our action.

*Krishnamurti's Talks 1949-1950 (Verbatim Report) ... Ceylon p.25*

6

When the mind is without activity, there is action; this action is without cause, and only then is there bliss.

*Commentaries on Living (First Series) p.242*

7

There is not first understanding and then action. When you understand, that very understanding is action.

*Talks by Krishnamurti in India 1965 p.102*

8

To see is to act. And if one does not see very clearly, naturally all action becomes confused. And we go to somebody else to tell us what to do; because we cannot see for ourselves what to do, clearly, precisely, all the time, all the days of our life, we resort to another to help us to see clearly.

*Talks by Krishnamurti in India 1966 p.6*

9

When you are *completely* attentive with *all* your being, in that state action is instantaneous.

*Talks by Krishnamurti in U.S.A. 1966 p.26*

# Aloneness

10

In those moments of complete aloneness, which only comes when all escapes and their significance have been truly discerned, is there the blessedness of the present.

*Reports of Talks and Answers to Questions ... New York City 1935 p.32*

11

He who is influenced is separate, knowing the division of the high and the low, of merit and demerit. Aloneness in the sense of being free from influence is not separative, not antagonizing. It is a state to be experienced, not speculated upon.

*Authentic Report of Sixteen Talks given in 1945 & 1946 ... p.108*

12

Very few of us are alone; we don't want to be alone. It is essential to understand that aloneness is not isolation. Surely, there is a difference between being alone, and isolation. Isolation is the sense of being enclosed, the sense of having no relationships, a feeling that you have been cut off from everything. That is entirely different from being alone, which is to be extraordinarily vulnerable.

*Krishnamurti's Talks 1949-1950 (Verbatim Report) ... Ceylon p.30*

13

Aloneness is not an isolation, it is not the opposite of loneliness; it is a state of being when all experience and knowledge are not.

*Krishnamurti's Talks 1949-1950 (Verbatim Report) ... India p.42*

14

Only to the alone can the causeless come, only to the alone is there bliss.

*Commentaries on Living (First Series) p.158*

15

There must be total freedom, which means that the mind must be capable of standing completely alone.

*Talks by Krishnamurti in Europe 1956 p.107*

16

The aloneness of which I am speaking is pure, incorruptible; it is free of all tradition, of all dogma and opinion, of everything that another has said. When the mind is in this state of aloneness, it is quiet, essentially still, not asking for anything; and such a mind is capable of knowing what is true.

*Talks by Krishnamurti in Europe 1956 p.107*

17

On the journey of life and death, you must walk alone; on this journey there can be no taking of comfort in knowledge, in experience, in memories. The mind must be purged of all the things it has gathered in its urge to be secure; its gods and virtues must be given back to the society that bred them. There must be complete, uncontaminated aloneness.

*Commentaries on Living (Third Series) p.64*

ANALYSIS *See* **Psychoanalysis**

# Atman (Soul)

18

You want permanency, and the Atman guarantees it.

*Krishnamurti's Talks 1949-1950 (Verbatim Report) ... India p.54*

19

Whether the Atman exists or not is merely a theory, a speculation, and speculation is a waste of time; it is for the sluggish, the thoughtless.

*Krishnamurti's Talks 1949-1950 (Verbatim Report) ... India p.54*

20

Thought creates the thinker, thought is always seeking a permanent state; seeing its own state of transition, of flux, of impermanence, thought creates an entity which it calls the thinker, the Atman, the Paramatman, the soul — a higher and higher security.

*Krishnamurti's Talks 1949-1950 (Verbatim Report) ... India p.65*

21

Everything about us, within as well as without — our relationships, our thoughts, our feelings — is impermanent, in a constant state of flux. Being aware of this, the mind craves permanency, a perpetual state of peace, of love, of goodness, a security that neither time nor events can destroy; therefore it creates the soul, the *Atman*, and the visions of a permanent paradise. But this permanency is born of impermanency, and so it has within it the seeds of the impermanent. There is only one fact: impermanence.

*Commentaries on Living (Third Series) p.253*

22

Is there a permanent thing in you? You are changing, your body changes, unless you are dead. Everything is in a movement, but you refuse to accept that movement. And to say there is a soul, an *atman*, means that thought has thought about it, or has invented it.

*Talks by Krishnamurti in India 1966 p.97*

23

You believe in an *atman*, because that is the popular thing, and it has been handed down through centuries; and you also like to believe that there is something very superior in you, which is permanent, which is divine and so on — which is all an intellectual concept and does not actually alter the ways of your life.

*Talks by Krishnamurti in India 1966 p.99*

## Attention

24

We must give our complete attention to the understanding of sorrow, and we cannot do this if we are trying to escape from sorrow, or if our minds are occupied in seeking the cause of it. There must be total attention, and not oblique concern.

*Commentaries on Living (Third Series) p.11*

25

Attention is not mechanical. You have to attend completely. When you, with all your being, attend to that sunset, without any emotion, without any sentiment, without any demand, then your mind, your brain, your body, your nerves — everything functions in complete union, and that state is attention. It cannot by any means be practised day after day, by looking at the sunset every day at a certain time, and saying, "I must put away my feelings, my sentiment, I must concentrate" — it will never take place.

*Talks by Krishnamurti in India 1966 p.36*

26

You cannot train yourself to be attentive. But you can be aware that you are inattentive. And when you are aware that you are inattentive, you are attentive.

*Talks by Krishnamurti in India 1966 p.54*

27

When there is self-knowledge, when there is delving deeply into the whole structure, the nature of oneself, then attention becomes a natural thing. There is great beauty in attention.

*Talks by Krishnamurti in U.S.A 1966 p.26*

28

When there is *complete* attention, there is no observer.

*Talks by Krishnamurti in U.S.A 1966 p.92*

## Austerity

29

Austerity does not lie in any outward symbol or act: wearing a loincloth or a monk's robe, taking only one meal a day, or living the life of a hermit. Such disciplined simplicity, however rigorous, is not austerity; it is merely an outward show without an inner reality. Austerity is the simplicity of inward aloneness, the simplicity of a mind that is purged of all conflict, that is not caught in the fire of desire, even the desire for the highest.

*Commentaries on Living (Third Series) p.23*

# Authority

30

The authority of another is blinding; only in utter freedom is the Supreme to be found.

*Authentic Report of Sixteen Talks given in 1945 & 1946 . . . p.60*

31

If sometimes we do not accept and obey symbols of outward authority we create our own inner authority, the subtle voice of our self.

*Authentic Report of Sixteen Talks given in 1945 & 1946 . . . p.65*

32

Beware of the man who says he knows.

*Authentic Report of Sixteen Talks given in 1945 & 1946 . . . p.65*

33

You must know for yourself, directly, the truth of yourself and you cannot realize it through another, however great. There is no authority that can reveal it.

*Authentic Report of Sixteen Talks given in 1945 & 1946 . . . p.85*

34

Authority is evil. Authority destroys, authority perverts, authority corrupts; and a man who follows authority, is destroying himself, and destroying also that which he has placed in a position of authority. The follower destroys the master, as the master destroys the follower.

*Krishnamurti's Talks Benares – India 1949 (Verbatim Report) p.37*

35

You yourself have to be the master and the pupil. The moment you acknowledge another as a master and yourself as a pupil, you are denying truth. There is no master, no pupil, in the search for truth.

*Krishnamurti's Talks Benares-India 1949 (Verbatim Report) p.37*

36

If you are very clear, if you are inwardly a light unto yourself, you will never follow anyone.

*Krishnamurti's Talks Benares – India 1949*
*(Verbatim Report) p.38*

37

The wise wield no authority, and those in authority are not wise.

*Education and the Significance of Life p.58*

38

Surely it is only the mind that is completely free from all conscious or unconscious authority, that is able to discover if there is any reality beyond the mere conceptions of the mind.

*Talks by Krishnamurti in Europe 1956 p.4*

39

When the mind is very clear, it needs no authority; but when it is uncertain, confused, when it is in misery, in turmoil, then it looks to another for help. And can another help? Or is there fundamentally no help at all, because the misery, the turmoil, the confusion, is created by oneself, and therefore must be cleared away by oneself? Surely, whatever another can do to help is but a temporary alleviation.

*Talks by Krishnamurti in Europe 1956 p.37*

40

One has to be both the teacher and the pupil oneself. That requires energy, attention, watchfulness; but we are lazy, and it is much easier to be told what to do. The man who tells you what to do you set up as your authority, and you become his slave; therefore you are never free, you are never a light unto yourself. So you invent the exploiter, and you become the exploited.

*Talks by Krishnamurti in Europe 1956 p.49*

41

I am not establishing myself as an authority to tell you what to do; because I do not believe in authority in spiritual matters. All authority is evil; and all sense of authority must cease, especially if we would find out what is God, what is truth, whether there is something beyond the mere measure of the mind.

*Talks by Krishnamurti in Europe 1956 p.69*

42

We may reject the authority of another, but unfortunately we still have the authority of our own experience, of our own knowledge, of our own thinking, and that in turn becomes the pattern which guides us; but that is essentially no different from the authority of another.

*Talks by Krishnamurti in Europe 1956 p.99*

43

We depend on authority because, among other things, we are afraid of not attaining salvation; and the mind that is dependent cannot know the immeasurable, that which is beyond all churches, all dogmas and beliefs.

*Talks by Krishnamurti in Europe 1956 p.107*

44

No authority knows; and he who knows cannot tell.

*Commentaries on Living (Third Series) p.214*

## Awareness

45

It is only through the flame of awareness, through full consciousness, not through self-analysis, that one can discern the prejudices, the escapes, the self-defensive values which are continually twisting experience.

*Reports of Talks and Answers to Questions ...*
*New York City 1935 p.28*

46

To understand, mind must delve deeply and yet it must know when to be alertly passive. It would be foolish and unbalanced to keep on digging without the recuperative and healing power of passivity. We search, analyze, look into ourselves, but it is a process of conflict and pain; there is no joy in it for we are judging or justifying or comparing. There are no moments of silent awareness, of choiceless passivity. It is this choiceless awareness, this creative passivity that is even more essential than self-observation and investigation. As the fields are cultivated, sown, harvested and allowed to lie fallow so must we live the four seasons in a day. If you cultivate, sow and harvest without giving rest to the soil it would soon become unproductive. The period of fallowness is as essential as tilling; when the earth lies fallow the winds, the rains, the sunshine bring to it creative productivity and it renews itself. So must the mind-heart be silent, alertly passive after travail, to renew itself.

*Authentic Report of Sixteen Talks given in 1945 & 1946 . . . p.16-17*

47

Self-awareness is arduous; to think-out, feel-out *every* thought-feeling is strenuous; but this awareness of every thought-feeling will bring to an end the wandering of the mind.

*Authentic Report of Sixteen Talks given in 1945 & 1946 . . . p.51*

48

Suppose you have collected letters for many years; now you look into the drawer and read letter after letter, keeping some and discarding others; what you keep you re-read and again you discard till the drawer is empty. Similarly, be aware of every thought-feeling, comprehend its significance, and should it return reconsider it for it has not been fully understood. As a drawer is useful only when empty so the mind must be free of all its accumulations for only then can there be that openness to wisdom and the ecstasy of the Real.

*Authentic Report of Sixteen Talks given in 1945 & 1946 . . . p.52*

49

Awareness is from moment to moment, it is not the cumulative effect of self-protective memories. Awareness is not determination nor is it the action of will. Awareness is the complete and unconditional surrender to what is, without rationalization, without the division of the observer and the observed. As awareness is non-accumulative, non-residual, it does not build up the self, positively or negatively. Awareness is ever in the present and so, non-identifying and non-repetitive; nor does it create habit.

*Authentic Report of Sixteen Talks given in 1945 & 1946 . . . p.100*

50

A tree is not merely the leaf, or the flower, or the fruit; it is also the branch, the trunk — it is everything that goes to make up the whole tree. Likewise, awareness is of the total process of the mind, not just of one particular segment of that process. But the mind cannot understand the total process of itself if it condemns or justifies any part, or identifies itself with the pleasurable and rejects the painful.

*Talks by Krishnamurti in Europe 1956 p.54*

51

You cannot keep a mechanism working at full speed all the time, it would break up; it must slow down, have rest. Similarly, we cannot maintain total awareness all the time. How can we? To be aware from moment to moment is enough. If one is totally aware for a minute or two, and then relaxes, and in that relaxation spontaneously observes the operations of one's own mind, one will discover much more in that spontaneity than in the effort to watch continuously.

*Talks by Krishnamurti in Europe 1956 p.55*

## 52

Just be aware; that is all what you have to do, without condemning, without forcing, without trying to change what you are aware of. Then you will see that it is like a tide that is coming in. You cannot prevent the tide from coming in; build a wall, or do what you will, it will come with tremendous energy. In the same way, if you are aware choicelessly, the whole field of consciousness begins to unfold. And as it unfolds, you have to follow: and the following becomes extraordinarily difficult — following in the sense to follow the movement of every thought, of every feeling, of every secret desire. It becomes difficult the moment you resist, the moment you say, "that is ugly" "this is good", "that is bad", "this I will keep", "that I will not keep".

So you begin with the outer and move inwardly. Then you will find, when you move inwardly that the inward and the outward are not two different things, that the outward awareness is not different from the inward awareness, and that they are both the same.

*Talks by Krishnamurti in India 1965 p.84-85*

53

It may last one second; you are *completely* aware for one second, and the next second you may be inattentive. But know also you *are* inattentive. Don't say, "Inattention must become attention"; thereby you introduce conflict, and in that conflict awareness and attention completely end.

*Talks by Krishnamurti in U.S.A 1966 p.87*

## Beauty

54

To understand beauty one must have an extraordinarily simple mind — that is, a mind unclouded by thought, that can look at things as they are, that can see the sunset with all the colour, loveliness and light, that can look at it simply, without verbalization and be in contact, in communion with it, without the word, without the gesture, without the memory, so that there is not "you" and the object which "you" are looking at.

That extraordinary communion without the object, without the thinker and the thought and the object and experience, that sense of immense space — that is beauty.

*Talks by Krishnamurti in India 1965 p.28*

55

Beauty is not a stimulant; it is not brought about, or put together, by architecture, by painting, by looking at the sunset, or by seeing a beautiful face. Beauty is something entirely different; it can only be understood when the experiencer is no longer there, and therefore experience ceases to exist.

*Talks by Krishnamurti in India 1966 p.29*

56

Beauty is not thought. The thing that is created by thought, is not beauty.

*Talks by Krishnamurti in India 1966 p.79*

# Becoming and Being

57

If the mind is seeking a result, however noble and worthy, if it is concerned with becoming it ceases to be extensive and infinitely pliable. It must be as the unknown to receive the Unknowable.

*Authentic Report of Sixteen Talks given in 1945 & 1946 . . . p.52*

58

We think that life is an endless ladder for us to climb ever to greater and greater heights. Our thinking-feeling is caught in the horizontal process of becoming; the becomer is ever accumulating, ever gaining, ever expanding. The self, the becomer, the creator of time, can never experience the Timeless. The self, the becomer, is the cause of conflict and sorrow.

*Authentic Report of Sixteen Talks given in 1945 & 1946 . . . p.74*

59

Being is only when there is no effort, positive or negative, to become; only when the becomer is self-aware and understands the enchaining sorrow and wasted effort of becoming and no longer uses will, then only can he be silent. His desire and his will have subsided; then only is there the tranquillity of supreme wisdom. To become non-greedy is one thing and being without greed is another; to become implies a process but being does not. Process implies time; the state of being is not a result, not a product of education, discipline, conditioning. You cannot transform noise into silence; silence can only come into being when noise ceases.

*Authentic Report of Sixteen Talks given in 1945 & 1946 . . . p. 74 - 75*

60

Becoming can never transform itself into Being. Becoming, the expansive and enclosing activity of the self, must cease; then there is Being. This Being cannot be thought about, cannot be imagined; the very thought about it is a hindrance; all that thought can do is to be aware of its own complex and subtle becoming, its own cunning intelligence and will.

*Authentic Report of Sixteen Talks given in 1945 & 1946 . . . p.116*

61

Becoming is the continuation of time, of sorrow. Becoming does not contain being. Being is always in the present, and being is the highest form of transformation. Becoming is merely modified continuity, and there is radical transformation only in the present, in being.

*Commentaries on Living (First Series) p.11*

62

During sleep, and often during waking hours, when becoming has entirely ceased, when the effect of a cause has come to an end, then that which is beyond time, beyond the measure of cause and effect, comes into being.

*Commentaries on Living (First Series) p.40*

63

Not to gather, but to die each day, each minute, is timeless being.

*Commentaries on Living (Second Series) p.159*

BEING *See* **Becoming and Being**

# Belief

64

For a man who is living fully, completely, for a man who is truly cultured, beliefs are unnecessary. He is creative. He is truly creative, and that creativeness is not the outcome of a reaction to a belief.

*Verbatim Reports of Talks and Answers . . Adyar, India 1933-34 p.29*

65

A man who lives by belief is not truly living; he is limited in his actions. But the man who, because he understands, is really free from belief and from the burden of knowledge, to him there is ecstasy, to him there is truth.

*Verbatim Reports of Talks and Answers . . .Adyar, India 1933-34 p.83*

66

The desire to believe should be understood and put away for it does not bring enlightenment.

*Authentic Report of Sixteen Talks given in 1945 & 1946 . . . p.72*

67

To believe is not to be religious; to have faith in something which is created by the mind is not to be open to the Real.

*Authentic Report of Sixteen Talks given in 1945 & 1946 . . . p.102-103*

68

Belief is an impediment to reality, and that is a very difficult pill to swallow for most of us. We are not seeking reality; we want gratification, and belief gives us gratification, it pacifies us.

*Krishnamurti's Talks 1949 - 1950 (Verbatim Report) . . . Ceylon p.23*

69

As medical knowledge helps to prevent physical pain, so beliefs help to prevent psychological pain, and that is why I am afraid of losing my beliefs, though I have no perfect knowledge or concrete proof of the reality of such beliefs.

*Krishnamurti's Talks 1949 - 1950 (Verbatim Report) . . . India p.38-39*

## Besant, Annie

70

Dr. Besant was our mother, she looked after us, she cared for us. But one thing she did not do. She never said to me, "Do this," or "Don't do that." She left me alone. Well, in these words I have paid her the greatest tribute.

*Verbatim Reports of Talks and Answers . . Adyar, India 1933-34 p.50*

## Brotherhood

71

As long as religion keeps men apart there can be no brotherhood, any more than there can be brotherhood as long as there is nationality, which must ever cause conflict among men.

*Verbatim Reports of Talks and Answers . . Adyar, India 1933-34 p.12*

72

If you had no divisions of beliefs, no sets of ideals, if you were really complete human beings, then there would be true brotherhood, true affection, not this artificial thing that you call brotherhood.

*Verbatim Reports of Talks and Answers .. .Adyar, India 1933-34 p.75*

CAUSE-EFFECT *See* **Karma**

# Ceremonies

73

If you are critical, questioning, why do you cling to ceremonies? Now do not compare one ceremony with another in order to decide which is the better, but find out if ceremonies are worthwhile at all. If you say, "The ceremonies which I perform are very satisfying to me," then I have nothing more to say. Your statement merely shows that you do not know of doubt. You are only concerned with being satisfied. Ceremonies keep people apart, and each believer in them says, "Mine are the best. They have more spiritual power than others." This is what the members of every religion, of every religious sect or society maintain, and over these artificial distinctions there have been quarrels for generations. These ceremonies and such other thoughtless barriers have separated man from man.

*Verbatim Reports of Talks and Answers* . . *Adyar, India 1933-34 p.30*

# Choice

74

There is choice when you choose a coat or a dress. But is there any other choice at all? Is there choice when you see something very clearly? For instance, when you see nationalism, which is rampant in the world, when you see what it entails, what is involved in it, the limitation, the quarrels, the battles, the pride and all the ugly business involved, which is poison, then, if you realize that it's poison, it drops away. There is no action; there is no choice. Choice exists only when there is confusion. When the mind is not confused, there is no choice. There is direct perception.

*Talks by Krishnamurti in U.S.A 1966 p.18*

# Comparison

75

Through approximation we think we are understanding, but is understanding born of comparison, judgment? Or is it the outcome of non-comparative thought? If you would understand something do you compare it with something else or do you study it for itself?

*Authentic Report of Sixteen Talks given in 1945 & 1946 ... p.8*

76

Do not be afraid that you will become sluggish, smug, self-contented if you do not compete in comparison. Once you have perceived the futility of comparison there is a great freedom. Then you are no longer striving to become but there is freedom to understand.

*Authentic Report of Sixteen Talks given in 1945 & 1946 ... p.8*

77

If you compare, approximate, you are being merely competitive, ambitious and your end then is success in which inherently is failure. Comparison implies a pattern of authority according to which you are measuring and guiding yourself. The oppression of authority cripples understanding. Comparison may produce a desired result but it is an impediment to self-knowledge.

*Authentic Report of Sixteen Talks given in 1945 & 1946 ... p.16*

78

When we listen to or experience something new our instinctive response is to compare it with the old, with a past experience, with a fading memory. This comparing gives strength to the past, distorting the present and so the new is ever becoming the past, the dead.

*Authentic Report of Sixteen Talks given in 1945 & 1946 ... p.72*

79

To live without comparison requires tremendous intelligence and sensitivity, because then there is no example, there is no something that *should be*, no ideal, no hero. We begin with what actually *is;* and to understand *what is*, there is no need for comparison. When we compare, we destroy *what is*.

*Talks by Krishnamurti in U.S.A 1966 p.33*

# Concentration

80

In trying to concentrate, the conflicting thoughts-feelings are suppressed or pushed aside or overcome and through this process there can be no understanding. Concentration is gained at the expense of deep awareness. If the mind is petty and limited, concentration will not make it any the less small and trivial; on the contrary it will strengthen its own nature. Such narrow concentration does not make the mind-heart vulnerable to Reality; it only hardens the mind-heart in its own obstinacy and ignorance and perpetuates the self-enclosing process.

*Authentic Report of Sixteen Talks given in 1945 & 1946 . . . p.52*

81

Any child is capable of concentration — give him a new toy and he is concentrated. Every business man is concentrated when he wants to make money. Concentration, which we think we should have in order to meditate, is really narrowness, a process of limitation, exclusion.

*Talks by Krishnamurti in Europe 1956 p.104*

82

The idea that we are distracted when we want to concentrate, only implies that you resist what you call distraction; but actually there is no distraction. When your thought wanders off, give your whole attention to that thought, don't call it distraction.

*Talks by Krishnamurti in India 1966 p.30*

## Concepts

83

As long as you have concepts, you never see what is true.

*Talks by Krishnamurti in U.S.A 1966 p.87*

# Conclusions

## 84

To come to a conclusion is to build a wall around oneself, a protective security which prevents understanding. Accumulated conclusions do not make for wisdom but only sustain the self. Without accumulation there is no self.

*Authentic Report of Sixteen Talks given in 1945 & 1946 ... p.107*

## 85

To jump to a conclusion, and to start thinking from that conclusion, prevents understanding and any further discovery.

*Commentaries on Living (Third Series) p.60*

# Conditioning

86

One may be able to reason very intelligently, very cleverly; but that reasoning has the background of a particular conditioning.

*Talks by Krishnamurti in Europe 1956 p.40*

87

The totality of our conditioning can be broken — not bit by bit, which takes time, but immediately, by directly perceiving the truth of the matter. It is the truth that liberates, not time, or your intention to be free.

*Talks by Krishnamurti in Europe 1956 p.41*

88

To say that the mind can or cannot be free from its conditioning, is still part of its conditioning; but to observe that conditioning without saying either, is a furthering of awareness — awareness of the whole process of thinking.

*Talks by Krishnamurti in Europe 1956 p.54*

89

To find out for oneself what is true, all influence must cease. There is no 'good' conditioning or 'bad' conditioning — there is only freedom from *all* conditioning.

*Talks by Krishnamurti in Europe 1956 p.104*

90

Having been brought up in a certain society, educated according to a particular ideology, with its dogmas and traditions, the mind is conditioned; and any movement of the mind to free itself, being the result of that conditioning, only leads to still further conditioning.

*Talks by Krishnamurti in Europe 1956 p.111*

# Confidence

91

This confidence may be called faith. It is not the faith of the foolish; it is not faith in something. Ignorance may have faith in wisdom, darkness in light, cruelty in love, but such faith is still ignorance. This confidence or faith of which I am speaking comes through experimentation in self-knowledge, not through acceptance and hope. The self-confidence that many have is the outcome of ignorance, of achievement, of self-glory or of capacity. The confidence of which I speak is understanding, not the *I understand,* but understanding without self-identification.

*Authentic Report of Sixteen Talks given in 1945 & 1946 . . . p.102*

92

Confidence comes into being, it cannot be manufactured by the mind; confidence comes with experiment and discovery; not the experiment with belief, theory or memory but experimentation with self-knowledge. This confidence or faith is not self-imposed nor is it identified with belief, formulation, hope. It is not the outcome of self-expanding desire.

*Authentic Report of Sixteen Talks given in 1945 & 1946 . . . p.103*

# Conflict

## 93

A mind that is in conflict and meets it without trying to interpret that conflict according to certain values becomes fully, completely aware. Then that mind and that heart shall awaken to the reality of life, the bliss of the present.

*Reports of Talks and Answers to Questions . . . New York City 1935 p.24*

## 94

Occasionally, in the still silence after the storm of conflict and pain, there comes inexpressible beauty and joy; it is not the result of the storm but of the cessation of conflict.

*Authentic Report of Sixteen Talks given in 1945 & 1946 . . . p.53*

## 95

A mind that is in conflict is a destructive mind, a wasteful mind, and those in conflict can never understand; but conflict is not stilled by any sanctions, beliefs, or disciplines, because the conflict itself has to be understood.

*Krishnamurti's Talks 1949-1950 (Verbatim Report) . . . India p.22*

96

Conflict is the denial of what *is* or the running away from what *is*; there is no conflict other than that. Our conflict becomes more and more complex and insoluble because we do not face what *is*.

*Commentaries on Living (First Series) p.217*

97

A life without friction is the religious life. And a mind without friction, without conflict is the religious mind. When that mind acts, it has every problem dissolved; it has no problem.

*Talks by Krishnamurti in India 1965 p.10*

98

You *can* live a life without conflict, which doesn't mean that you become a vegetable. On the contrary, the mind then becomes highly aware, intelligent, full of energy, passion. Conflict dissipates this intelligence.

*Talks by Krishnamurti in U.S.A 1966 p.33*

# Consciousness

99

Consciousness is the product of the mind and the mind is the result of conditioning, of craving, and so it is the seat of the self. Only when the activity of the self, of memory, ceases is there a wholly different consciousness, about which any speculation is a hindrance. The effort to expand is still the activity of the self whose consciousness is to grow, to become. Such consciousness however expanded is time-binding and so the Timeless is not.

*Authentic Report of Sixteen Talks given in 1945 & 1946 . . . p.87*

## 100

There is in fact only one state, not two states such as the conscious and the unconscious; there is only a state of being, which is consciousness, though you may divide it as the conscious and the unconscious. But that consciousness is always of the past, never of the present; you are conscious only of things that are over. You are conscious of hearing me the second it is over, are you not?; you understand it a moment later. You are never conscious or aware of the now. Watch your own hearts and minds and you will see that consciousness is functioning between the past and the future, and that the present is merely a passage of the past to the future.

*Krishnamurti's Talks 1949-1950 (Verbatim Report) . . . India p.72*

101

To be an integrated human being is to understand the entire process of one's own consciousness, both the hidden and the open.

*Education and the Significance of Life p.65*

102

To expand consciousness there must be a center which is aware of its expansion. The moment there is a center from which you are expanding, it is no longer expansion because the center always limits its own expansion.

*Talks by Krishnamurti in U.S.A 1966 p.41*

103

You can observe the *whole* field, what is called the unconscious *and* the conscious, which are on that field, only when there is no observer at all, when there is no attempt to change what *is*, when you are totally attentive, completely attentive of the whole field. Then you will find out for yourself that there is no such thing as the unconscious, and there is nothing to be examined.

*Talks by Krishnamurti in U.S.A 1966 p.87*

# Contentment

104

Contentment with little comes with the understanding of our psychological problems, not through legislation or the determined effort to possess little. We must eliminate intelligently those psychological demands which find gratification in things, in position, in capacity. If we do not seek power and domination, if we are not self-assertive, there will be peace; but as long as we are using things, relationship or ideas as means to gratify our ever increasing psychological cravings, so long will there be contention and misery.

*Authentic Report of Sixteen Talks given in 1945 & 1946 . . . p.49*

## 105

A mind that is becoming can never know the full bliss of contentment; not the contentment of smug satisfaction, not the contentment of an achieved result, but the contentment that comes when the mind sees the truth in what is and the false in what is.

*Krishnamurti's Talks Benares - India 1949 (Verbatim Report) p.40*

## 106

Contentment, which is not the opposite of discontent, is that state in which there is the understanding of what *is*; and the understanding of what *is* is not a matter of time, it is not in the movement of the past to the future. The mind can be free only when it is simple, clean, and such a mind alone can be content.

*Krishnamurti's Talks 1949-1950 (Verbatim Report) ... India p.53*

## 107

Contentment and discontent are like the two sides of one coin. To be free from the ache of discontent, the mind must cease to seek contentment.

*Commentaries on Living (Third Series) p.76*

# Creation

108

Only when the mind ceases to create is there creation.

*Authentic Report of Sixteen Talks given in 1945 & 1946 . . . p.54*

109

Creation is one of the most difficult things to understand. The man who writes a poem, however beautiful, thinks he is a creative being. The man and the woman who breed children think that they are creative. The man or the cook who makes bread thinks, perhaps, he is also creative. But creation is something far more. That man is not creative, who merely writes a book or fulfils himself in some petty little ambition. Creation is not a man-made structure, or man-made technological knowledge and the result of technological knowledge which is merely invention. Creation is something that is timeless, that has no tomorrow and yesterday; it is: living timelessly.

*Talks by Krishnamurti in India 1965 p.48*

# Culture

110

Culture is universal. True culture is infinite; it does not belong to any one society, to any one nation, to any one religion. A true artist is neither Hindu nor Christian, American nor English, for an artist who is conditioned by tradition or by nationalism is not a true artist.

*Verbatim Reports of Talks and Answers . . .Adyar, India 1933-34 p.28*

# Death

111

We cling to the pleasant and let the unpleasant go; so we strengthen in gratification and know death. Without seeking reward, let us abandon our gatherings and then only can there be the immortal. Then life is not opposed to death nor is death a darkening of life.

*Authentic Report of Sixteen Talks given in 1945 & 1946 . . . p.35*

112

Die to the whole of our existence, not little by little, but totally!

*Commentaries on Living (Third Series) p.106*

113

To die to everything that you have learnt is to learn. This dying is not a final act: it is to die from moment to moment.

*Commentaries on Living (Third Series) p.247*

114

The man who takes the *sanyasi's* robes, grows a beard, goes to the temple and runs away from life — he is not a religious man. The religious man is one who dies every day and is reborn every day. That is, his mind is young, innocent, fresh. To die to your sorrow, die to your pleasure, die to the things that you hold secretly in your heart — do it; thus you will see you will not waste your life; then you will find something that is incredible, that no man has ever perceived. This is not a reward. There is no reward either. You die willingly, or you die inevitably.

*Talks by Krishnamurti in India 1965 p.79*

## 115

Death is not the end of life. Death is not an event brought about by disease, by senility, by old age, or by accident. Death is something that you live every day with, because you are dying every day to everything that you know.

*Talks by Krishnamurti in India 1965 p.92*

## 116

There is the death of the physical organism; and to find out what is beyond that, can the whole psyche, with all the tendencies, pleasures, idiosyncrasies, memories, experiences, die each day, *completely*, without argument, without restraint — just die?

*Talks by Krishnamurti in U.S.A 1966 p.31*

## 117

Death means a renewal, a total mutation, in which thought does not function at all, because thought is the old. But when there is death, there is something totally new.

*Talks by Krishnamurti in India 1966 p.103*

# Discipline

118

Discipline can only build walls about us; it is always exclusive, ever making for conflict. Discipline is not conducive to understanding; for understanding comes with observation, with inquiry in which all prejudice is set aside.

*Education and the Significance of Life p.32*

119

It is intelligence that brings order, not discipline.

*Education and the Significance of Life p.33*

# Discontent

120

A man who is complacent, a man who is satisfied with money, with position, with an idea, can never see truth. It is only the man who is discontented, who is investigating, who is asking, questioning, looking, that discovers truth, and such a person is a revolution in himself and therefore in his relationships.

*Krishnamurti's Talks Benares - India 1949 (Verbatim Report) p.6*

121

You cannot seek reality, it must come to you; but it can only come to you when the mind is completely discontented and ready.

*Krishnamurti's Talks Benares - India 1949 (Verbatim Report) p.7*

122

Truth comes to him who is in that state of discontent, but who does not seek an end; for the seeker of an end is the person who is seeking gratification; and gratification, satisfaction, is not truth.

*Krishnamurti's Talks Benares - India 1949*
*(Verbatim Report) p.7*

123

A mind that is completely discontented can jump into reality; not a mind that is content, not a mind that is respectable, hedged about by beliefs.

*Krishnamurti's Talks Benares - India 1949*
*(Verbatim Report) p.15*

124

That timeless state can come only when there is a tremendous discontent — not the discontent that has found a channel through which it escapes, but the discontent that has no outlet, that has no escape, that is no longer seeking fulfillment. Only then, in that state of supreme discontent can reality come into being.

*Krishnamurti's Talks Benares - India 1949*
*(Verbatim Report) p.40*

125

The young, if they are at all alive, are full of hope and discontent; they must be, otherwise they are already old and dead. And the old are those who were once discontented, but who have successfully smothered that flame and have found security and comfort in various ways.

*Education and the Significance of Life p.41*

126

Discontent may bring what appears to be disorder; but if it leads, as it should, to self-knowledge and self-abnegation, then it will create a new social order and enduring peace.

*Education and the Significance of Life p.42*

127

Though painful, it is a marvellous thing to be discontented without smothering that flame with knowledge, with tradition, with hope, with achievement.

*Commentaries on Living (Second Series) p.151*

# Disease

128

If we are organically diseased then let us cope with this condition as with all mechanism, in the best way possible. The psychological delusions, tensions, conflicts, maladjustments produce greater misery than organic disease. We try to eradicate symptoms rather than cause; the cause itself may be sensate value. There is no end to the gratification of the senses which only creates greater and greater turmoil, tension, fear and so on; such a living must culminate in mental and physical disorder or in war.

*Authentic Report of Sixteen Talks given in 1945 & 1946 . . . p.54*

# Doubt

129

Doubt brings about lasting understanding; doubt is not an end in itself. What is true is revealed only through doubt, through questioning the many illusions, traditional values, ideals.

*Verbatim Reports of Talks and Answers . . .Adyar, India 1933-34 p.29*

130

If you doubt, that is, if you desire greatly to find out, you must let go of those things which you hold so dearly. There cannot be true understanding by keeping what you have. You cannot say, "I shall hold on to this prejudice, to this belief, to this ceremony, and at the same time I shall examine what you say." How can you? Such an attitude is not one of doubt; it is not one of intelligent criticism.

*Verbatim Reports of Talks and Answers . . .Adyar, India 1933-34 p.30*

131

For understanding, the first requirement is doubt, doubt not only with regard to what I say, but primarily with regard to the ideas which you yourselves hold. But you have made an anathema of doubt, a fetter, an evil to be banished, to be put away; you have made of doubt an abominable thing, a disease. But to me, doubt is none of these; doubt is an ointment that heals.

*Verbatim Reports of Talks and Answers . . Adyar, India 1933-34 p.80*

132

You doubt what the other says. It is very easy to doubt someone else. But to doubt the very thing in which you are caught up, that you hold, to doubt the very thing that you are seeking, pursuing, that is more difficult.

*Verbatim Reports of Talks and Answers . . Adyar, India 1933-34 p.80*

# Dreams

133

The more there is an awareness of the conscious layers the more the hidden layers come to the surface; if the conscious layers are confused and disturbed then the deeper layers of consciousness cannot project themselves into the conscious, save through dreams.

*Authentic Report of Sixteen Talks given in 1945 & 1946 . . . p.52*

134

Through constant awareness the dreamer ceases to dream, for through alert and passive awareness every movement of thought-feeling of the open and hidden layers of consciousness is being understood. But if one is incapable of thinking-out, feeling-out every thought completely and fully then one begins to dream. Dreams need interpretation and to interpret there must be free and open intelligence; instead, the dreamer goes to a dream specialist, thus creating for himself other problems. Only in deep extensive awareness can there be an end to dreams and their anxious interpretation.

*Authentic Report of Sixteen Talks given in 1945 & 1946 . . . p.53*

135

It has become the fashion to inquire into the unconscious. Whereas, if we are at all aware of the whole field, there is no need for the unconscious at all; and therefore there is no need for dreams. It is only the mind that is aware of a particular corner of the field and totally unaware of the rest that begins to dream; and then there are all the interpretations of dreams, and all that stuff. If we are aware during the entire day of every thought, every feeling, every motive, every response — aware, not interpreting it, not condemning it, not justifying it, but just being aware of the whole process — then we will see that there is no need for dreams at all.

*Talks by Krishnamurti in U.S.A 1966 p.28*

136

When one is aware, watching all things, choicelessly; looking, not interpreting, then you will find for yourself that you don't dream at all, because you have understood everything as you are going along.

*Talks by Krishnamurti in U.S.A 1966 p.87*

DUALITY *See* **Thought and Thinker**

# Education

137

To understand life is to understand ourselves, and that is both the beginning and the end of education. Education is not merely acquiring knowledge, gathering and correlating facts; it is to see the significance of life as a whole.

*Education and the Significance of Life p.14*

138

Without goodness and love, you are not rightly educated.

*Commentaries on Living (Third Series) p.113*

# Effort

139

Illumination, understanding of the Real, can never come through the expansion of the self, through the I making an effort to grow, to become, to achieve and there is no effort apart from the will of the I.

*Authentic Report of Sixteen Talks given in 1945 & 1946 . . . p.87*

140

All effort we now make issues from the desire for self-expansion; only when there is an effortless awareness can there be discovery and understanding, a perception of the true.

*Authentic Report of Sixteen Talks given in 1945 & 1946 . . . p.93*

141

It is truth that frees, not your effort to be free.

*Authentic Report of Sixteen Talks given in 1945 & 1946 . . . p.102*

142

Effort is the very denial of understanding; and it is only the quiet mind, the simple mind, the mind that is still, that is not overtaxed by its own efforts — only such a mind shall understand, shall see truth.

*Krishnamurti's Talks 1949-1950 (Verbatim Report) ... India p.99*

143

It is only when effort ceases that you have an unbounding energy inwardly, so that your mind remains crystal clear and can tackle any human problem.

*Talks by Krishnamurti in India 1966 p.111*

EGO *See* **Self**

# Emptiness

144

The emptying of the mind is not a slow process; but *trying* to empty it is a hindrance.

*Krishnamurti's Talks 1949-1950 (Verbatim Report) ... India p.35*

145

To know your own emptiness, you must look at it; but you cannot look at it if your mind is all the time seeking a distraction from the fact that it is empty.

*Talks by Krishnamurti in Europe 1956 p.53*

146

Is it possible to empty the whole of consciousness, the whole of the mind, with all its tricks and vanities, its deceptions, pursuits and moralities, and all that, based essentially on pleasure? Is it possible to be totally free of it all, to empty the mind so that it can look and act and live totally differently? I say that it is possible, but not out of vanity or some superstitious, mystical nonsense. It is possible only when there is a realization that the observer, the center is the observed.

*Talks by Krishnamurti in U.S.A 1966 p.7*

147

It's only when the cup is empty that it can be filled. It is only when the mind and heart are totally empty that they can comprehend; then they can live. But to be so completely empty is not a negative phenomenon. On the contrary, it is the highest form of intelligence. It is the highest form of love to be so completely empty that there is not a scratch of memory, not a word, not a conclusion that distorts perception.

*Talks by Krishnamurti in U.S.A 1966 p.74*

148

When the mind is completely empty, being silent, it is capable of renewing itself entirely without any outside pressures, circumstances; then it is something clear, pristine and there is a joy which is not pleasure.

*Talks by Krishnamurti in India 1966 p.103*

# Energy

149

One needs abundant energy to find truth, and this energy is dissipated through the conflict which results from suppression, conformity, compulsion. But yielding to desire also breeds self-contradiction, which again dissipates energy.

*Commentaries on Living (Third Series) p.294*

150

The desire to conserve energy is greed. This essential energy cannot be conserved or accumulated; it comes into being with the cessation of contradiction within oneself.

*Commentaries on Living (Third Series) p.294*

151

I do not know if you have seen a machine or a dynamo, something that is moving with terrific speed, full of energy. In the same way the mind that is completely silent is completely full of energy. And that energy, because it is not named, has no nationality, no conflict. That energy is anonymous; it is not yours or mine. And therefore that energy, when allowed to move freely, goes very far; it can go beyond the measure of time.

*Talks by Krishnamurti in India 1965 p.87*

152

This energy, this intensity, this vitality does not come by gathering energy; but through the very act of investigation there is energy, through the very act of enquiry energy comes.

*Talks by Krishnamurti in India 1965 p.115*

## Envy

153

If I try to free myself from envy by cultivating a state of mind in which there is no envy, I am still envious, because the drive to cultivate a state of non-envy is based on envy.

If I would eradicate the feeling called 'envy', I must understand this whole problem, so that the mind can dissociate itself from all words, including that particular word 'envy' . And if it does, *is* there envy? But merely getting rid of the word as a clever trick in order not to be envious, does not bring about a mind that is completely still, without a word.

*Talks by Krishnamurti in Europe 1956 p.49*

# Escapes

## 154

The search for the beyond is merely an escape from what *is;* and if you *want* to escape, then religion or God is as good an escape as drink. Don't object to this putting drink and God on the same level. *All* escapes are on the same level, whether you escape through drink, through *puja,* or whatever it be.

*Krishnamurti's Talks 1949-1950 (Verbatim Report) . . . India p.21*

## 155

A man who is happy, who loves, does not want possessions, he is not carried away by success, by power, position or authority. It is the unhappy, the sorrowful, who seek power and success as an escape from their own insufficiency.

*Krishnamurti's Talks 1949-1950 (Verbatim Report) . . . India p.53*

## 156

Reality is what you are, what you do, what you think, and your belief in God is merely an escape from your monotonous, stupid and cruel life.

*Krishnamurti's Talks 1949-1950 (Verbatim Report) . . . India p.75*

157

Most of us are constantly trying to escape from ourselves; and as art offers a respectable and easy means of doing so, it plays a significant part in the lives of many people. In the desire for self-forgetfulness, some turn to art, others take to drink, while still others follow mysterious and fanciful religious doctrines.

When, consciously or unconsciously, we use something to escape from ourselves, we become addicted to it. To depend on a person, a poem, or what you will, as a means of release from our worries and anxieties, though momentarily enriching, only creates further conflict and contradiction in our lives.

*Education and the Significance of Life p.120*

## Experience

158

If you have lived an experience fully, completely, have you not found that it leaves no traces behind? It is only the incomplete experiences that leave their mark, giving continuity to self-identified memory.

*Authentic Report of Sixteen Talks given in 1945 & 1946 . . . p.53*

159

As each experience arises live it out as fully and deeply as possible; think it out, feel it out extensively and profoundly; be aware of its pain and pleasure, of your judgments and identifications. Only when experience is completed is there a renewal. We must be capable of living the four seasons in a day; to be keenly aware, to experience, to understand and be free of the gatherings of each day. With the end of each day the mind-heart must empty itself of the accumulation of its pleasures and pains. We gather consciously and unconsciously; it is comparatively easy to discard what has been consciously acquired but it is more difficult for thought to free itself from the unconscious accumulations, the past, the incompleted experiences with their recurring memories. Thought-feeling clings so tenaciously to what it has gathered because it is afraid to be insecure.

*Authentic Report of Sixteen Talks given in 1945 & 1946 . . . p.54*

160

If the experiencer has an experience, there is no longer the state of experiencing. It is the experiencing of what *is* without naming it that brings about freedom from what *is*.

*Commentaries on Living (First Series) p.54*

161

Experiencing is a very strange thing. The moment you know you are experiencing, there is the cessation of that experience. The moment I know I am happy, I am no longer happy. To experience this immeasurable reality, the experiencer must come to an end. The experiencer is the result of the known, of many centuries of cultivated memory; he is an accumulation of the things he has experienced. So when he says "I must experience reality", and is cognizant of that experience, then what he experiences is not reality, but a projection of his own past, his own conditioning.

*Talks by Krishnamurti in Europe 1956 p.68*

162

Unless one is highly enlightened, intelligent and sensitive, man is kept awake through experience, through challenge. And you must receive every experience and not retain a shadow of it afterwards.

*Talks by Krishnamurti in U.S.A 1966 p.77*

163

A quiet mind, a still mind, never experiences. It is only the observer that experiences. Therefore it is not a still mind.

*Talks by Krishnamurti in U.S.A 1966 p.87*

FAITH *See* **Grace and Faith**

# Fear

164

Your craving for security creates fear and it is fear that yields to the oppression of authority; fear forces you not *how* to think but *what* to think. Only in freedom from fear is there the discovery of the Real.

*Authentic Report of Sixteen Talks given in 1945 & 1946 . . . p.58*

165

Fear can exist only in relation to something, it is not in isolation. How can I be afraid of death, how can I be afraid of something I do not know? I can be afraid only of what I know. When I say I am afraid of death, am I really afraid of the unknown, which is death, or am I afraid of losing what I have known? My fear is not of death, but of losing my association with things belonging to me.

My fear is always in relation to the known, not to the unknown.

*Krishnamurti's Talks 1949-1950 (Verbatim Report) . . . India p.38*

166

Fear perverts intelligence and is one of the causes of self-centered action.

*Education and the Significance of Life* p.34

167

Fearlessness brings independence without ruthlessness, without contempt for another, and this is the most essential factor in life.

*Education and the Significance of Life* p.46

168

Fear dulls the mind and heart so that we are not alert to the whole significance of life; we become insensitive to our own sorrows, to the movement of the birds, to the smiles and miseries of others.

Conscious and unconscious fear has many different causes, and it needs alert watchfulness to be rid of them all. Fear cannot be eliminated through discipline, sublimation, or through any other act of will: its causes have to be searched out and understood. This needs patience and an awareness in which there is no judgment of any kind.

*Education and the Significance of Life* p.57

169

It is in the very process of running away from what *is* that fear arises.

*Talks by Krishnamurti in Europe 1956 p.53*

170

Only the mind that is inwardly free of fear can know the blessing of reality; and the mind can be free of fear only when there is no dependence.

*Talks by Krishnamurti in Europe 1956 p.92*

171

The mind is always afraid of coming to an end.

*Commentaries on Living (Second Series) p.22*

172

One is afraid of the inner aloneness, the sense of emptiness, that might arise if the mind no longer had something to cling to; so there is attachment to an ideology, a belief, which prevents the understanding of what *is*.

*Commentaries on Living (Third Series) p.281*

173

Fear is the product of thought. Fear in every form is thought in action with regard to the past through the present and to the future. I am afraid of what will happen, and I'm afraid of something which I have done in the past which I want to cover up. So thought, fear is the movement of time; and it's very important, if we would be free of fear, to understand this movement of time, which is essentially the process of thinking.

*Talks by Krishnamurti in U.S.A 1966 p.75*

## Freedom

174

Freedom is not at the end, liberation is not an end product; it must be at the beginning, otherwise you cannot discover.

*Krishnamurti's Talks 1949-1950 (Verbatim Report) ... India p.54*

175

There can be no compromise with freedom. Partial freedom for the individual is no freedom at all.

*Education and the Significance of Life p.39*

176

The man who is free is not free *for* something, or *from* something; he is just free; and then if that state of reality wishes to come, it will come.

*Talks by Krishnamurti in Europe 1956 p.22*

177

The moment we struggle against bondage, we create another bondage. But if we can understand the whole psychological process of bondage — not merely what binds us now, but how it has come into being, the motives, the implications, the whole background of it, both conscious and unconscious — then in that very understanding there is freedom; we do not have to 'become' free.

*Talks by Krishnamurti in Europe 1956 p.38*

178

If you are free *from* something, that freedom is merely a reaction and therefore it is not freedom. Please understand this — not intellectually, but feel your way into it. If I am free from anger, that freedom from anger — not being angry any more — is another form of resistance, another form of suppression or sublimation, and therefore it is not real freedom. Freedom means: freedom in itself, and not from something.

*Talks by Krishnamurti in India 1965 p.138*

# God

179

Out of an opinion or a belief the mind can project an idea or an image of God; but it is a projection of itself, of its own chatter, of its own fabrication, and therefore it is not real.

*Krishnamurti's Talks 1949-1950 (Verbatim Report) ... India p.20*

180

If you have proof of the existence of God, then it is not God; (laughter) because proof is of the mind. How can the mind prove or disprove God? Therefore your god is a projection of the mind according to your satisfaction, appetite, happiness, pleasure or fear.

*Krishnamurti's Talks 1949-1950 (Verbatim Report) ... Ceylon p.19-20*

181

A man who believes in God can never find God. If you are open to reality, there can be no belief in reality. If you are open to the unknown, there can be no belief in it. After all, belief is a form of self-protection, and only a petty mind can believe in God.

*Krishnamurti's Talks 1949-1950 (Verbatim Report) ... Ceylon p.27*

182

The mind is the product of the past, it is the result of yesterday; and can such a mind be open to the unknown? It can only project an image, but that projection is not real; so your god is not God, it is an image of your own making, an image of your own gratification.

*Krishnamurti's Talks 1949-1950 (Verbatim Report) ... Ceylon p.27*

183

Neither the believer nor the non-believer will find God; because, reality is the unknown, and your belief or non-belief in the unknown is merely a self-projection and therefore not real.

*Krishnamurti's Talks 1949-1950 (Verbatim Report) ... India p.74*

184

God is not the word, the word is not the thing. To know that which is immeasurable, which is not of time, the mind must be free of time, which means the mind be free from all thought, from all ideas about God.

*Krishnamurti's Talks 1949-1950 (Verbatim Report) ... India p.75*

185

So long as there is the 'me' who wants to experience, there can be no experiencing of reality. That is why the experiencer — the entity who is seeking God, who believes in God, who prays to God — must totally cease. Only then can that immeasurable reality come into being.

*Talks by Krishnamurti in Europe 1956 p.68*

186

To find out that ultimate reality which man has called God for thousands upon thousands of years, you must be free from belief; you must be free from authority. Then only can you find out if there is such a thing as God.

*Talks by Krishnamurti in U.S.A 1966 p.41*

## Grace and Faith

187

How is this revolution to take place? As we do not know, we say that we must have faith, or that grace must descend upon us. This may be so: grace may come. But the faith that is cultivated is only another creation of the mind, and therefore it can be destroyed. Whether there is grace or not, is not our concern; a mind that *seeks* grace will never find it.

*Talks by Krishnamurti in Europe 1956 p.64*

# Greed

188

A greedy mind is a conflicting mind; a greedy mind is ever fearful, envious in its self-growth and fulfillment. Such a mind is ever changing the objects of its desire and this changing is considered growth; a greedy mind which renounces the world in order to seek Reality, God, is still greedy; greed is ever restless, ever seeking growth, fulfillment, and this restless activity creates self-assertive intelligence but is not capable of understanding the Real.

Greed is a complex problem! To live in the world of greed without greed needs deep understanding; to live simply, earning a right livelihood in a world organized on economic aggression and expansion is possible only for those who are discovering inward riches.

*Authentic Report of Sixteen Talks given in 1945 & 1946 . . . p.103*

189

The greed for Reality is the same as the greed for possessions.

*Authentic Report of Sixteen Talks given in 1945 & 1946 ... p.114*

## Gurus

190

There is no need to go from teacher to teacher, from guru to guru, from leader to leader, for all things are contained in you, the beginning and the end.

*Authentic Report of Sixteen Talks given in 1945 & 1946 ... p.112*

191

When we choose a *guru* out of our confusion, that *guru* must also be confused, otherwise we wouldn't choose him. To understand yourself is essential, and a *guru* who is worthy of that name must obviously tell you that. But to most of us, this is a tiresome business; we want quick relief, a panacea, so we turn to a *guru* who will give us a satisfactory pill. We are searching not for truth but for comfort; and the man who gives us comfort, enslaves us.

*Krishnamurti's Talks 1949-1950 (Verbatim Report) ... Ceylon p.5*

192

You must understand it, go into it, examine it, give your heart and your mind, with everything that you have, to find out a way of living differently. That depends on you, and not on someone else, because in this there is no teacher, no pupil; there is no leader; there is no *guru*; there is no Master, no Saviour. You yourself are the teacher and the pupil; you are the Master; you are the *guru*; you are the leader; you are everything.

*Talks by Krishnamurti in U.S.A 1966 p.73*

## Habit

193

Habit is mechanical, and to resist it is only to feed the machine, give more power to it. But if you consider the mind and observe the formation of its habits, then with the understanding of the larger issue, the lesser becomes insignificant and drops away.

*Commentaries on Living (Third Series) p.285*

194

The mind forms habits in order to be secure, safe, certain, undisturbed, in order to have continuity. Memory is habit.

*Commentaries on Living (Third Series) p:285*

## Happiness

195

Happiness is not something that is gained by position, prestige, it is not arrived at through any means. We say we are happy because we have money, a position, or some means of sensation; but surely, that is not happiness. Happiness is a state of being in which there is no dependence; for where there is dependence there is fear, and a man who is fearful can never be happy, however much he may cover up his fear.

*Krishnamurti's Talks 1949-1950 (Verbatim Report) . . . India p.67*

196

A happy man does not follow. It is the miserable, the confused man who eagerly pursues another, hoping for refuge; and he will find a refuge, but that refuge is his darkness, it is his undoing. It is only the man who tries to find out the fact of what he is in himself that will know freedom and therefore happiness.

*Krishnamurti's Talks 1949-1950 (Verbatim Report) . . . India p.68*

197

Happiness is not an end in itself. It comes with the understanding of what *is*. Only when the mind is free from its own projections can there be happiness. Happiness that is bought is merely gratification; happiness through action, through power, is only sensation; and as sensation soon withers, there is craving for more and more. As long as the more is a means to happiness, the end is always dissatisfaction, conflict and misery. Happiness is not a remembrance; it is that state which comes into being with truth, ever new, never continuous.

*Commentaries on Living (Second Series) p.71*

# Humility

198

If you cultivate humility, you are only covering up your vanity. Humility is something that must blossom naturally.

*Talks by Krishnamurti in India 1966 p.28*

# Ideals

199

The ideal is an escape from what you are.

*Krishnamurti's Talks 1949-1950 (Verbatim Report) ... India p.21*

200

Ideals and blue-prints for a perfect Utopia will never bring about the radical change of heart which is essential if there is to be an end to war and universal destruction. Ideals cannot change our present values: they can be changed only by the right kind of education, which is to foster the understanding of what *is*.

*Education and the Significance of Life p.21*

201

Ideals are merely a means of postponing, an excuse to avoid bringing about a real change. So long as we have an ideal, there is always a conflict between what *is* and what *should* be, and we spend a great deal of energy in this inward conflict, through which we hope to bring about a fundamental change. If we are envious, we set up the ideal of non-envy, hoping thereby to free the mind from envy. But if you examine closely this whole process, you will see that the ideal actually prevents the understanding of what *is*, which is envy. So the ideal is not important, it is an impediment, a thing to be put away completely.

*Talks by Krishnamurti in Europe 1956 p.12-13*

202

The ideal is fictitious, ego-made, and becoming the ideal is an escape from what *is*.

*Commentaries on Living (Second Series) p.6*

# Imagination

203

Imagination has no place in meditation; it must be completely set aside, for the mind caught in imagination can only breed delusions. The mind must be clear, without movement, and in the light of that clarity the timeless is revealed.

*Commentaries on Living (Third Series) p.10*

# Immortality

204

Immortality can be known only when thinking ceases, when through understanding, the process of thought comes to an end.

*Krishnamurti's Talks 1949-1950 (Verbatim Report) . . . Ceylon p.19*

# Individuality

205

You are the result of your past and present environment, and what you express, calling it individuality or self-expression, is nothing but the expression of that conditioning environment. To me, the true expression of individuality is that intelligence which is awakened through freeing the mind from the conditioning environment of the past and the present.

*Reports of Talks and Answers to Questions . . . New York City 1935 p.9*

INSECURITY *See* **Security**

# Inspiration

206

Have you not noticed that inspiration comes when you are not seeking it? It comes when all expectation has ceased, when the mind-heart is still.

*Authentic Report of Sixteen Talks given in 1945 & 1946 . . . p.34*

207

Why do we seek inspiration? As our lives are empty, dull and mechanical we seek inspiration outside of ourselves. The Master, the saint, the savior then becomes a necessity, a necessity which enslaves us. Being enslaved you then have to free yourself from your enchainment to discover the Real, for the Real can only be experienced in freedom.

Because you are *not* interested in self-knowledge you seek from others inspiration which is another form of distraction. Self-knowledge is a process of creative discovery which is hindered when thought-feeling is concerned with gain. Greed for a result prevents the flowering of self-knowledge. Search itself is devotion, it is in itself inspiration.

*Authentic Report of Sixteen Talks given in 1945 & 1946 . . . p.77*

208

Mind has the power to create illusion; and without understanding its ways, to seek inspiration is to invite self-deception. Inspiration comes when we are open to it, not when we are courting it. To attempt to gain inspiration through any form of stimulation leads to all kinds of delusions.

*Education and the Significance of Life p.121*

## Intelligence

209

The very essence of intelligence is to understand life or experience with an unburdened mind and heart, anew, afresh.

*Reports of Talks and Answers to Questions ...*
*New York City 1935 p.24*

210

It is only when we face experience as it comes and do not avoid disturbance that we keep intelligence highly awakened; and intelligence highly awakened is intuition, which is the only true guide in life.

*Education and the Significance of Life p.11*

211

There is a distinction between intellect and intelligence. Intellect is thought functioning independently of emotion, whereas, intelligence is the capacity to feel as well as to reason; and until we approach life with intelligence, instead of intellect alone, or with emotion alone, no political or educational system in the world can save us from the toils of chaos and destruction.

*Education and the Significance of Life p.63-64*

212

Intelligence is much greater than intellect, for it is the integration of reason and love; but there can be intelligence only when there is self-knowledge, the deep understanding of the total process of oneself.

*Education and the Significance of Life p.65*

213

Intelligence is the spontaneous perception which makes a man strong and free.

*Education and the Significance of Life p.103*

214

Intelligence is not the accumulation of experience and knowledge; but intelligence is the highest form of sensitivity. To be sensitive to everything, to the birds, to the squalor, to the poverty, to the beauty of a tree, to the beauty of a face, to the sunset, to the colours, to the reflections, to the movement of a leaf, to a bird on the wing, to the smile of a child, to tears, to laughter, to the pain, the agony, the anguish, the misery of a human being — to be totally sensitive to all that means to be intelligent.

*Talks by Krishnamurti in India 1965 p.23*

# Joy and Pleasure

215

With self-abnegation comes immeasurable joy.

*Education and the Significance of Life p.42*

## 216

Pleasure has a continuity; joy has not. When we say, "I am joyful", it's already finished, but pleasure you can continue. Therefore pleasure is a continuity of that which was, which gave you gratification or pleasure yesterday, which, through thought, you can continue today, tomorrow and sustain it. Whereas joy is something that comes immediately, naturally, and goes away naturally, but if you cling to it, it has already become a memory, a pleasure.

*Talks by Krishnamurti in U.S.A 1966 p.72-73*

## 217

Thought creates pleasure. I think about something that has given me pleasure for a moment; and the more I think about it, the more I give strength to that pleasure.

*Talks by Krishnamurti in India 1966 p.111*

# Karma

218

Cause and effect are inseparable; in the cause is the effect. To be aware of the cause-effect of a problem needs certain swift pliability of mind-heart for the cause-effect is constantly being modified, undergoing continual change. What once was cause-effect may have become modified now and to be aware of this modification or change is surely necessary for true understanding. To follow the ever changing cause-effect is strenuous for the mind clings and takes shelter in what was the cause-effect; it holds to conclusions and so conditions itself to the past. There must be an awareness of this cause-effect conditioning; it is not static but the mind is when it holds fast to a cause-effect that is immediately past. Karma is this bondage to cause-effect. As thought itself is the result of many causes-effects it must extricate itself from its own bondages.

*Authentic Report of Sixteen Talks given in 1945 & 1946 . . . p.62*

219

Karma is the process of time, the past moving through the present to the future; this chain is the way of thought. Thought is the result of time, and there can be that which is immeasurable, timeless, only when the process of thought has ceased.

*Commentaries on Living (Second Series) p.80*

220

Karma is not an ever-enduring chain; it's a chain that can be broken at any time. What was done yesterday can be undone today; there's no permanent continuance of anything. Continuance can and must be dissipated through the understanding of its process.

*Commentaries on Living (Third Series) p.280*

# Knowledge

221

Search to understand, not to know; for in understanding, the dual process of the knower and the known ceases. In the mere search for knowledge the knower is ever becoming and so is ever in conflict and sorrow. He who asserts he knows does not know.

*Authentic Report of Sixteen Talks given in 1945 & 1946 . . . p.72*

222

To know is to be ignorant; not to know is the beginning of wisdom.

*Commentaries on Living (First Series) p.210*

223

Only the mind which is capable of being in a state of not-knowing — not merely as a verbal assertion, but as an actual fact — is free to discover reality. But to be in that state is difficult, for we are ashamed of not knowing. Knowledge gives us strength, importance, a centre around which the ego can be active.

*Talks by Krishnamurti in Europe 1956 p.21*

224

Identification with the knowledge we have gained is another way of furthering the self, is it not? Through knowledge the 'me' continues its struggle to be something, and thereby perpetuates misery, pain.

*Talks by Krishnamurti in Europe 1956 p.75*

# Learning

225

To a mind that's learning, the heavens are open.

*Commentaries on Living (Third Series) p.247*

226

You can only learn if you listen. And listening is an act of silence; it is only the mind that is very quiet but tremendously active, that can learn.

*Talks by Krishnamurti in India 1965 p.11*

227

The learning process is always going on, infinitely. But if one has learnt and then adds to it what one is learning, then learning ceases.

*Talks by Krishnamurti in India 1966 p.23*

# Liberation

228

Liberation is not an end. Liberation is from moment to moment in the understanding of what *is* — when the mind is free, not *made* free.

*Krishnamurti's Talks 1949-1950 (Verbatim Report) ... India p.22*

229

For the attainment of liberation, nothing is *necessary*. You cannot attain it through bargaining, through sacrifice, through elimination; it is not a thing that you can buy. If you do these things you will get a thing of the marketplace, therefore not real.

*Krishnamurti's Talks 1949-1950 (Verbatim Report) ... Ceylon p.12*

230

Listening to the story of what *is* brings its own liberation. It is truth that liberates, not the effort to be free.

*Commentaries on Living (First Series) p.171*

## Listening

231

We listen either with pleasure, with distaste, or with a formula of ideas, a philosophy which we have cultivated, or have learned. Through these screens we listen, interpreting, translating, putting aside what we don't like, keeping what we like, and the act of listening never takes place.

*Talks by Krishnamurti in U.S.A 1966 p.27*

# Livelihood

232

Obviously there are wrong means of livelihood. He who helps in manufacturing arms and other methods to kill his fellowman is surely occupied with furthering violence which never brings about peace in the world; the politician who, either for the benefit of his nation or of himself or of an ideology, is occupied in ruling and exploiting others, is surely employing wrong means of livelihood which lead to war, to the misery and sorrow of man; the priest who holds to a specialized prejudice, dogma or belief, to a particular form of worship and prayer is also using wrong means of livelihood, for he is only spreading ignorance and intolerance which set man against man. Any profession that leads to and maintains the divisions and conflict between man and man is obviously a wrong means of livelihood. Such occupations lead to exploitation and strife.

*Authentic Report of Sixteen Talks given in 1945 & 1946 . . . p.17*

233

It is very important in modern society to have right employment, because today every action leads to war, the whole thing is geared for war; but at least we can find out the wrong professions; and avoid them intelligently. Obviously, the army, the navy, are wrong professions; so is the profession of law which encourages litigation, and the police, especially the secret police. So, right employment must be found and exercised by each one, and only then can there be the cessation of killing which will bring about peace among men.

*Krishnamurti's Talks 1949-1950 (Verbatim Report) ...*
*Ceylon p.15*

## Loneliness

234

We try to escape from loneliness through companionship, through work, amusement, worship, prayer, all the well known and cunningly well established escapes. Why do we do that? We think that we can cover up loneliness by these escapes, through these releases. Can we ever cover up a thing that is inherently diseased? We may momentarily cover up loneliness, but it continues all the time.

*Reports of Talks and Answers to Questions ...*
*New York City 1935 p.15*

235

When you are lonely, be fully aware and you will see that your mind wants to run away, wants to escape. When the mind is aware that it is escaping and at the same time perceives the absurdity of escape, in that understanding loneliness truly disappears.

*Reports of Talks and Answers to Questions . . . New York City 1935 p.15*

236

To find the right and lasting answer to loneliness we must first cease to run away from it, and this is very difficult for thought is ever seeking a refuge, an escape. It is only when the mind-heart can accept this void unconditionally, yielding to it without any motive, without any hope or fear, that there can be its transformation.

*Authentic Report of Sixteen Talks given in 1945 & 1946 . . . p.46*

# Love

237

Love has no motive; it is its own eternity.

*Authentic Report of Sixteen Talks given in 1945 & 1946 . . . p.57*

238

If you observe, what makes us stale in our relationship, is thinking, thinking, thinking, calculating, judging, weighing, adjusting ourselves; and the one thing which frees us from that, is love, which is not a process of thought. You cannot *think* about love. You can think about the person whom you love, but you cannot think about love.

*Krishnamurti's Talks Benares - India 1949 (Verbatim Report) p.18*

239

Love is not personal or impersonal; it is *love*, it has no frontiers, it has no class, race. A man who loves is revolutionary, he alone is revolutionary.

*Krishnamurti's Talks Benares - India 1949 (Verbatim Report) p.18*

240

We shall know that state of love only when jealousy, envy, possessiveness, domination, come to an end; and as long as we possess, we shall never love.

*Krishnamurti's Talks 1949-1950 (Verbatim Report) ... India p.97*

241

The things of the mind are jealousy, envy, ambition, the desire to be somebody, to achieve success. These things of the mind fill your hearts, and then you say you love; but how can you love when you have all these confusing elements in you? When there is smoke, how can there be a pure flame? Love is not a thing of the mind; and love is the only solution to our problems.

*Krishnamurti's Talks 1949-1950 (Verbatim Report) ... India p.98*

242

Only when you put away the things of the mind, only when your hearts are empty of the things of the mind, is there love. Then you will know what it is to love without separation, without distance, without time, without fear — and that is not reserved to the few. Love knows no hierarchy, there is only love. There are the many and the one, an exclusiveness, only when you do not love. When you love, Sir, there is neither the 'you' nor the 'me', in that state there is only a flame without smoke.

*Krishnamurti's Talks 1949-1950 (Verbatim Report) . . . India p.98*

243

The man who knows how to split the atom but has no love in his heart becomes a monster.

*Education and the Significance of Life p.19*

244

Without love, you cannot wipe out the past; with love, there is no past.

*Commentaries on Living (First Series) p.146*

245

The action of love has no motive, and every other action has.

*Commentaries on Living (Third Series) p.60*

246

With love everything is possible.

*Commentaries on Living (Third Series) p.155*

247

This sense of affection, this love, this quality cannot be cultivated, cannot be practised, cannot be brought about; but it must happen as naturally as breathing, as fully with great joy and delight as the sunset.

*Talks by Krishnamurti in India 1965 p.36*

248

Love is: dying every day. Love is not memory, love is not thought. Love is not a thing that continues as duration in time. And, through observation, one must die to the continuity of everything. Then there is love; and with love, there comes creation.

*Talks by Krishnamurti in India 1965 p.48*

249

If you have no love, do what you will — go after all the gods on earth, do all the social activities, try to reform the poor, the politics, write books, write poems — you are a dead human being. And without love your problems will increase, multiply endlessly. And with love, do what you will, there is no risk; there is no conflict. Then love is the essence of virtue. And a mind that is not in a state of love, is not a religious mind at all.

*Talks by Krishnamurti in India 1965 p.73*

250

To love somebody, an animal, a human being, a tree, the sky, the open space — when you love something, what does it mean? It means, surely, not intellection, not the reaction of memory, but an intensity between two individuals or between two objects, an intensity at the same level and at the same time; then there is a communication, non-verbal, non-intellectual, non-sentimental. Love is not sentiment, love is not emotion, love is not devotion.

*Talks by Krishnamurti in India 1966 p.28*

# Mantra Yoga

251

The repetition of chants, of words and phrases, puts the mind to sleep, though it is stimulating enough for the time being. In this sleepy state, experiences do occur, but they are self-projected. However gratifying, these experiences are illusory. The experiencing of reality does not come about through any repetition, through any practice.

*Commentaries on Living (First Series) p.24-25*

252

Meditation is not what is done all the world over: repetition of words, sitting in a certain posture, breathing in a certain way, repeating some *sloka* or *mantram* over and over again. Naturally that makes the mind stupid, dull; and out of that stupidity, dullness, the mind becomes silent and you think you have got silence. That kind of meditation is merely self-hypnosis. It is not meditation at all. It is the most destructive way of meditating.

*Talks by Krishnamurti in India 1966 p.113*

# Meditation

253

Meditation is not for a set period only but is to be continued during the waking hours and hours of sleep as well. In sleep, because of right meditative awareness during waking hours, thought can penetrate depths that have great significance. Even in sleep meditation continues.

*Authentic Report of Sixteen Talks given in 1945 & 1946 . . . p.68*

254

Meditation is not the cultivation of the becomer but through self-knowledge the meditator, the becomer ceases.

*Authentic Report of Sixteen Talks given in 1945 & 1946 . . . p.75*

255

Meditation is the purgation from the mind of all its accumulations; the purgation of the power to gather, to identify, to become; the purgation of self-growth of self-fulfillment; meditation is the freeing of the mind from memory, from time.

*Authentic Report of Sixteen Talks given in 1945 & 1946 . . . p.115*

256

When the meditator understands himself and comes to an end, only then is there meditation; for the ending of the meditator is meditation.

*Krishnamurti's Talks 1949-1950 (Verbatim Report) ... India p.29*

257

Meditation is that silence which comes into being when the meditator and his processes are understood. That silence is inexhaustible; it is not of time, therefore it is immeasurable. Only the meditator compares, judges, measures; but when the measurement is not, the immeasurable is.

*Krishnamurti's Talks 1949-1950 (Verbatim Report) ... India p.29*

258

Without meditation there is no perfume to life, no beauty, no love.

*Talks by Krishnamurti in Europe 1956 p.104*

259

If there is a deliberate act of meditation, then it becomes an effort, and therefore a pressure on the mind. So, meditation is not a deliberate act, it is not a continuity. Because the moment it has continuity, it has time-value; and therefore, it has been created by the mind as a means to achieve something, or as a means to retain something. So meditation is an act which ends each minute and has no continuity.

*Talks by Krishnamurti in India 1965 p.86*

# Memory

260

Anything that we perceive directly, understand completely, leaves no scar on the mind. If you live in an experience wholly, although you may recall the incident, it will not produce those reactions which you use for your self-defense. If I have an experience whose significance I do not completely understand, then mind but becomes a centre of conflict and this conflict continues till I understand that experience wholly. As long as the mind is burdened with these conflicts, it is but a storehouse of defensive reactions, called memories, and with such protective memories we approach life, thus creating a barrier between life and ourselves, from which ensues all conflict, fear and suffering.

*Reports of Talks and Answers to Questions ...*
*New York City 1935 p.17-18*

261

Memory, as the identifying process, gives continuity to the self. Memory then is an enclosing, hindering activity. On it the whole structure of the ego, the I, is built. We are considering psychological memory not the memory for speech, facts, for the development of technique and so on.

*Authentic Report of Sixteen Talks given in 1945 & 1946 . . . p.116*

262

The mind is full of memories, it is made up of memories. You have no mind without memory — the memories of your past, of all the things you have learnt, experienced, lived, suffered. Mind is memory, conscious or unconscious. In memory there is the pleasant and the unpleasant, and we want to reject the unpleasant; we want to keep the desirable, and get rid of the undesirable, so there is always a conflict going on. What we have to understand is not how to retain the pleasant and be free of the terrible memories, but rather how to eliminate the desire to keep some memories and reject others, which creates conflict. What is important is to be aware of this conflict, and to understand why it is that the mind gathers memories and holds on to them.

*Talks by Krishnamurti in Europe 1956 p.72*

263

If you had no memories of the pleasant, of the hopeful, of the enjoyable, of the things that you have lived for, you would feel non-human, you would feel lost, a nobody. The mind clings to its pleasant memories, because without them it would be lonely, in despair.

*Talks by Krishnamurti in Europe 1956 p.72*

264

Memory is only the past, and anything born of memory is always old, never new. To discover something totally new, the mind must be astonishingly quiet, still, not active, not desiring and reacting to memories.

*Talks by Krishnamurti in Europe 1956 p.73*

# Mind

265

The questioner wants to know how my mind works. If I may go into it a little, I will show you. There is no centre from which it is acting, there is no memory from which it is responding. There is memory of the road which I took just now, of the road where I live, there is the recognition of people, of incidents; but there is no accumulating process, no mechanical process of gradual gathering, from which comes response. If I did not know the usage of English or some other language, I would not be able to speak. Communication on the verbal level is necessary in order to understand each other; but it is what is said, how it is said, from where it is said, that is important. Now, when a question is put, if the answer is the response of a mind which has accumulated experiences and memories, then it is merely reaction, and therefore it is not reasoning; but when there is no accumulation, which means no response, then there is no frustration, no effort, no struggle. The accumulating process, the accumulating centre, is like a deep-rooted tree in a stream which gathers debris around itself; and thought, sitting on the top of that tree, imagines it is thinking, living. Such a mind is only accumulating, and the mind which accumulates, whether knowledge, money, or experience, is obviously not living. It is only when the mind moves, flows, that there is living.

*Krishnamurti's Talks 1949-1950 (Verbatim Report) ... India p.91*

266

The very nature of our mind is to be dishonest, crooked, incapable of facing facts, and that is the thing which creates problems, that is the thing which is the problem itself.

*Krishnamurti's Talks 1949-1950 (Verbatim Report) ... India p.94*

267

The mind is an astonishing instrument; there is no man-made machinery that is so complex, subtle, with such infinite possibilities.

*Commentaries on Living (Second Series) p.240*

268

The mind can never be great, for what is great is immeasurable.

*Commentaries on Living (Second Series) p.241.*

# Mutation

269

To look without the interference of the past is to look in complete silence. And out of that silence comes about a mutation, not thought out, not planned, not conditioned. And it is only such a mutation that can bring about order in the world.

*Talks by Krishnamurti in India 1965 p.106*

270

All mutation is instantaneous.

*Talks by Krishnamurti in India 1966 p.23*

271

It seems to me that there must be a total change, a total revolution in the mind, not a modified continuity, but a total psychological mutation, so that the mind is entirely free from all the bondage of time, so that it can go beyond the structure of thought, not into some metaphysical region, but rather into a timeless dimension where the mind is no longer caught in its own structure, in its own problems.

*Talks by Krishnamurti in U.S.A 1966 p.12*

272

Ideas and words never bring about a radical revolution, a mutation in the mind.

*Talks by Krishnamurti in U.S.A 1966 p.68*

# Mystery

273

There is a mystery that is beyond the capacities and powers of the mind. You cannot seek it out or invite it; it must come without your asking, and with it comes a benediction for man.

*Commentaries on Living (Second Series) p.151*

# Nationalism

274

Nationalism always produces war, and the problem is not to be solved by bringing about further nationalism, which is only an avoidance of the fact and an extension of the same poison, but by being free of nationalism, of the sense of belonging to a particular group, to a particular class or society.

*Krishnamurti's Talks 1949-1950 (Verbatim Report) ... India p. 104*

275

The separative spirit of nationalism is spreading like fire all over the world. Patriotism is cultivated and cleverly exploited by those who are seeking further expansion, wider powers, greater enrichment; and each one of us takes part in this process, for we also desire these things. Conquering other lands and other people provides new markets for goods as well as for political and religious ideologies.

*Education and the Significance of Life* p.69-70

276

Nationalism, the patriotic spirit, class and race consciousness, are all ways of the self, and therefore separative. After all, what is a nation but a group of individuals living together for economic and self-protective reasons? Out of fear and acquisitive self-defence arises the idea of "my country", with its boundaries and tariff walls, rendering brotherhood and the unity of man impossible.

*Education and the Significance of Life* p.70

277

It is because we are nationalists, ready to defend our sovereign States, our beliefs and acquisitions, that we must be perpetually armed. Property and ideas have become more important to us than human life, so there is constant antagonism and violence between ourselves and others. By maintaining the sovereignty of our country, we are destroying our sons; by worshipping the State, which is but a projection of ourselves, we are sacrificing our children to our own gratification. Nationalism and sovereign governments are the causes and the instruments of war.

*Education and the Significance of Life p.71*

## Nothingness

278

We must break through our own conditioning and be as nothing.

*Authentic Report of Sixteen Talks given in 1945 & 1946 . . . p.43*

279

You are nothing. You may have your name and title, your property and bank account, you may have power and be famous; but in spite of all these safeguards, you are as nothing. You may be totally unaware of this emptiness, this nothingness, or you may simply not want to be aware of it; but it is there, do what you will to avoid it.

*Commentaries on Living (First Series) p.92*

280

The man who is as nothing is without fear, without ambition; he is alone, but not isolated.

*Talks by Krishnamurti in Europe 1956 p.7*

## Observation

281

When you observe a tree, if you have ever done it, when you look at a tree, your mind never observes the tree; it observes the image it has created about a tree; and that image is always moving; it is never quiet. It is being added to and taken away from. It is only when the mind is very quiet, really observant, without any movement, that it observes the actual fact of the tree.

*Talks by Krishnamurti in U.S.A 1966 p.62*

282

To look, there must be freedom from the image. And when you are free, you look, not with the intellect, not with emotion, but with love, with clarity, with something totally new.

*Talks by Krishnamurti in India 1966 p.95*

OCCUPATION *See* **Livelihood**

## Opinions

283

Surely, opinions, values, interpretations, merely prevent the mind from looking at the fact. If you want to understand the fact, it is no good having an opinion about it.

*Talks by Krishnamurti in Europe 1956 p.53*

284

Surely, to know love, truth, God, there must be no opinions, no beliefs, no speculations with regard to it. If you have an opinion about a fact, the opinion becomes important, not the fact. If you want to know the truth or the falseness of the fact, then you must not live in the word, in the intellect.

*Commentaries on Living (Third Series) p.214*

285

You know, it's only fools who offer opinions. The wise man has no opinions.

*Talks by Krishnamurti in U.S.A 1966 p.72*

## Organisations

286

Do not be lost and confused in organizations but remain wholly alone and simple.

*Authentic Report of Sixteen Talks given in 1945 & 1946 ... p.15*

287

If certain ideas, beliefs, doctrines appeal to you, you join with others to spread effectively what you believe and for this you create an organization. But is the understanding of Reality the result of propaganda, organized belief, enforced or subtle conformity? Is Reality discovered through the doctrines of churches, cults or sects? Is Reality to be found through compulsion, through imitation?

*Authentic Report of Sixteen Talks given in 1945 & 1946 ... p.58*

288

If one belongs to an organization which demands belief, which is based on fear, on dogma, then the mind is a slave to that organization and cannot be free.

*Talks by Krishnamurti in Europe 1956 p.17*

289

Why do you belong to any particular religious organization? We must obviously have organizations to deliver letters, milk, and so on; but why does the mind cling to dogmas? Does it not cling because in dogma, in belief, it finds security, something to rely on? Being uncertain, fearful, insecure, it projects a belief or clings to a dogma that some church or other organization offers.

*Talks by Krishnamurti in Europe 1956 p.17*

# Peace

290

You must pay the price for peace. You must pay it voluntarily and happily and the price is the freedom from lust and ill-will, worldliness and ignorance, prejudice and hate. If there were such a fundamental change in you, you could help to bring about a peaceful and sane world. To have peace you must be compassionate and thoughtful.

*Authentic Report of Sixteen Talks given in 1945 & 1946 ... p.15*

291

It is only when you have no reason for being peaceful that you will have peace.

*Krishnamurti's Talks 1949-1950 (Verbatim Report) ... India p.63*

292

A mind that invents a reason for being peaceful is in conflict, and such a mind will produce chaos and conflict in the world.

*Krishnamurti's Talks 1949-1950 (Verbatim Report) ... India p.63*

293

Peacefulness, that state of peace, is not stagnation; on the contrary, it is a most active state. But the mind can only know the activity of its own creation, which is thought; and thought can never be peaceful, thought is sorrow, thought is conflict.

*Krishnamurti's Talks 1949-1950 (Verbatim Report) . . .*
*India p.63*

294

Peace is a state of being in which all conflicts and all problems have ceased; it is not a theory, not an ideal to be achieved after ten incarnations, ten years or ten days. As long as the mind has not understood its own activity, it will create more misery; and the understanding of the mind is the beginning of peace.

*Krishnamurti's Talks 1949-1950 (Verbatim Report) . . .*
*India p.64*

295

If you want peace in the world you have to live peacefully, not hating each other, not being envious, not seeking power, not pursuing competition. Because out of that freedom from these you have love. It is only a mind that is capable of loving, that will know what it is to live peacefully.

*Talks by Krishnamurti in India 1965 p.121*

296

Peace and freedom are absolutely essential, because nothing can grow, function fully, completely, except in peace, and there can be no peace without freedom.

*Talks by Krishnamurti in India 1966 p.7*

297

The idea that there should be peace in the world is an ideation, which has no reality. There is no peace in the world because as a human being I'm aggressive, competitive, ambitious, dividing myself into different groups, sociologically, morally and spiritually.

*Talks by Krishnamurti in U.S.A 1966 p.18*

# Perception

298

Probably there must be the capacity to see the truth in a flash — and I think that very perception will cleanse the mind of all the past in an instant.

*Talks by Krishnamurti in Europe 1956 p.65*

299

It seems to me that what each one of us has to do is to capture the significance of the totality of our thinking. But much concern over detail, over the many conflicting thoughts and feelings, will not bring about an understanding of the whole. What is required is the sudden perception of the totality of the mind — which is not the outcome of asking *how* to see it, but of constantly looking, inquiring, searching.

*Talks by Krishnamurti in Europe 1956 p.65*

300

The state of the mind which is really inquiring into the capacity of total perception is one of complete humility, complete stillness; and this very humility, this stillness, is that capacity itself.

*Commentaries on Living (Third Series) p.127*

# Philanthropy

301

We want to be rich; and the richer we get, the more ruthless we become, even though we may contribute large sums to charity and education. Having robbed the victim, we return to him a little of the spoils, and this we call philanthropy.

*Education and the Significance of Life p.78*

PLEASURE *See* **Joy and Pleasure**

# Possessiveness

302

If we cannot see the falseness of possessiveness immediately, we shall then not be able individually, and therefore collectively, to have a different civilization, a different way of living.

*Reports of Talks and Answers to Questions . . .New York City 1935 p.29*

## 303

You know, in India we have certain people called *sannyasis*, who leave the world in search of truth. They have generally two loin cloths, the one they put on, and one for the next day. A *sannyasi* in search of truth, sought various teachers. In his wanderings he was told that a certain king was enlightened, that he was teaching wisdom. So this *sannyasi* went to the king. You can see the contrast between the king and the *sannyasi*: the king who had everything, palaces, jewels, courtiers, power; and the *sannyasi* who had only two loin cloths. The king instructed him concerning truth. One day, while the king was teaching him, the palace caught fire. Serenely the king continued with his teaching, while the *sannyasi*, that holy man, was greatly disturbed because his other loin cloth was burning.

You know, you are all in that position. You may not be possessive with regard to clothes, houses, friends, but there is some hidden pursuit of gain to which you are attached, to which you cling, which is eating your hearts and minds away. As long as these unexplored, hidden poisons exist, there must be continual conflict, suffering.

*Reports of Talks and Answers to Questions . . .New York City 1935 p.29*

304

Suppose you are possessive. Don't say to yourself, "Well, I have heard this afternoon that I mustn't be possessive, so I will get rid of that desire." Don't develop a contradictory resistance. If you are possessive, be completely and wholly aware of it; then you will see what happens.

*Reports of Talks and Answers to Questions ...New York City 1935 p.31*

305

Can there be love where there is possessiveness? Can we be in communion with those whom we seek to control? To dominate is to use another for self-gratification, and where there is the use of another there is no love.

*Education and the Significance of Life p.48*

# Prayer

## 306

Do you pray when you are joyous, when you are happy, when there is no confusion, no misery? You pray when there is misery, when there is disturbance, fear, turmoil, and your prayer is supplication, petition. When you are in misery, you want somebody to help you out, a higher entity to give you a helping hand; and that process of supplication in different forms is called prayer. So, what happens? You put out your begging bowl to someone, it does not matter who it is — an angel, or your own projection whom you call God. The moment you beg, you have something — but whether that something is real or not, is a different question. You want your confusion, your miseries solved; so you get out your traditional phrases, you turn on your devotion, and the constant repetition obviously makes the mind quiet. But that is not quietness — the mind is merely dulled and put to sleep. In that induced quiet, when there is supplication there is an answer. But it is not at all an answer from God — it is from your own ornamental projection.

*Krishnamurti's Talks 1949-1950 (Verbatim Report) . . . Ceylon p.20*

307

Receptivity is the capacity to be open, without condemnation or justification, to what *is*; and it is *that* from which you try to escape through prayer.

*Krishnamurti's Talks 1949-1950 (Verbatim Report) ... Ceylon p.20*

## Problems

308

If we can approach our problem without judging, without identifying, then the causes that lie behind it are revealed. If we would understand a problem we must set aside our desires, our accumulated experiences, our patterns of thought. The difficulty is not in the problem itself but in our approach to it. The scars of yesterday prevent the right approach. Conditioning translates the problem according to its own pattern, which in no way liberates thought-feeling from the struggle and pain of the problem. To translate the problem is not to understand it; to understand it and so transcend it interpretation must cease.

*Authentic Report of Sixteen Talks given in 1945 & 1946 ... p.45*

309

To solve a problem is not to search for an answer, a solution. If my mind is concerned with the solution of the problem, then I have created another problem, have I not?

*Talks by Krishnamurti in Europe 1956 p.55*

310

Thinking about the problem is escape from the problem; for thinking *is* the problem, and the only problem.

*Commentaries on Living (Second Series) p.6*

311

There is no separate problem by itself; every problem is inter-related with another problem. So, a mind that seeks to solve a particular problem will never solve it, because that particular problem is related to half-a-dozen other problems, conscious as well as unconscious. It is only a religious action that can solve all problems altogether.

*Talks by Krishnamurti in India 1965 p.9*

312

Look! When the mind faces a problem, it is always seeking a way out, by trying to solve it, to overcome it, to go round it or beyond it or above it — by always doing something with the problem, moving out or within. If it did not move in any direction — when there is no movement at all, within or without, but there is only the problem — then there would be an explosion in that problem.

*Talks by Krishnamurti in India 1965 p.93*

313

A problem exists only when there is an inadequate response to the challenge; otherwise we have no problem. When we are incapable of responding totally to a challenge, whatever that challenge may be, then, out of that inadequacy, we have a problem. These challenges being always new, we respond to them mechanically, or with the accumulation of knowledge or experience, and there is no immediate response.

*Talks by Krishnamurti in U.S.A 1966 p.35*

PROFESSION *See* **Livelihood**

# Progress

314

Existence which was simple and primitive has become very complex, highly organized and civilized. We have "progressed"; we have radios, movies, quick means of transportation and all the rest of it. We can kill, instead of a few, thousands upon thousands in a moment; we can wipe out, as the phrase goes, whole cities and their people in a few burning seconds. We are well aware of all this and some call it progress; bigger and better houses, more luxury, more amusements, more distractions. Can this be considered progress? Is the expansion of sensate desire progress? Or does progress lie in compassion?

We mean by progress also, do we not, the constant expanding of desire, of the self? Now in this process of expansion and becoming can there ever be an end to conflict and sorrow? If not, what is the purpose of becoming? If it is for the continuation of struggle and pain, of what value is progress, the evolution of desire, the expansion of the self? If in the expansion of desire there is the cessation of sorrow then becoming could have significance, but is it not the very nature of craving to create and continue conflict and sorrow?

*Authentic Report of Sixteen Talks given in 1945 & 1946 ... p.60*

# Psychoanalysis

315

You may understand certain events, certain experiences; but the whole content of consciousness cannot be emptied through the analytical process. It can be emptied only when you see the falseness of the approach through analysis. When you see the false as the false, then you begin to see what is true; and it is truth that is going to liberate you from the background.

*Krishnamurti's Talks Benares – India 1949 (Verbatim Report) p.12*

316

In analysis there is always the possibility of misinterpretation, and the question of whether the analyser himself is free.

*Talks by Krishnamurti in Europe 1956 p.28*

317

You may not got to a psychoanalyst, you may analyse yourself, but in either case there is always the analyser and the analysed. When you try to examine the unconscious, or interpret a dream, there is the examiner and the examined; and the examiner, the interpreter, analyses what he sees in terms of his own background, according to his pleasure. So there is always a division between the analyser and the analysed, with the analyser trying to reshape or control that which he has analysed. And the question is not only whether the analyser is capable of analysing, but more fundamentally whether there is actually any division between the analyser and the analysed. We have assumed that there *is* such a division; but is there in actuality? The analyser, surely, is also the result of our thinking. So really there is no division at all, but we have artificially created one.

*Talks by Krishnamurti in Europe 1956 p.112*

# Reality

318

This inward freedom of creative Reality is not a gift; it is to be discovered and experienced. It is not an acquisition to be gathered to yourself to glorify yourself. It is a state of being, as silence, in which there is no becoming, in which there is completeness. This creativeness may not necessarily seek expression; it is not a talent that demands an outward manifestation.

*Authentic Report of Sixteen Talks given in 1945 & 1946 . . . p.18*

319

Is not Reality ever the uncreated? And must not the mind cease to create, to formulate, if it would experience the Uncreated?

*Authentic Report of Sixteen Talks given in 1945 & 1946 . . . p.26*

320

Reality is to be experienced, not speculated upon. This experience can only be when the mind-heart ceases to accumulate.

*Authentic Report of Sixteen Talks given in 1945 & 1946 . . . p.35*

321

You may not invite Reality, it must come to you; you may not choose Reality, it must choose you.

*Authentic Report of Sixteen Talks given in 1945 & 1946 . . . p.38*

322

The mind that seeks security through the Real creates only illusion. The Real is not a refuge; it is not the reward for righteous action; it is not an end to be gained.

*Authentic Report of Sixteen Talks given in 1945 & 1946 . . . p.64*

323

As the mind is ever seeking to expand through its own creations it cannot experience Reality. If the mind, the instrument, is blurred, it is of little use in the search of truth. It must first cleanse itself and then only will it be possible to know if there is Reality.

*Authentic Report of Sixteen Talks given in 1945 & 1946 . . . p.88*

324

The Real is Causeless and thought that has cause cannot experience it.

*Authentic Report of Sixteen Talks given in 1945 & 1946 . . . p.113*

325

That reality is not to be bought, to be sold, to be repeated; it cannot be caught in books. It has to be found from moment to moment, in the smile, in the tear, under the dead leaf, in the vagrant thoughts, in the fullness of love.

*Krishnamurti's Talks Benares - India 1949 (Verbatim Report) p.40*

326

Reality is not to be spoken of; and when it is, it is no longer reality.

*Commentaries on Living (First Series) p.45*

327

That immense reality cannot be found through any organization, through any church, through any book, through any person or teacher. One has to find it for oneself — which means that one has to be completely alone, uninfluenced.

*Talks by Krishnamurti in Europe 1956 p.76*

## Reform

328

Reform, however necessary, only breeds the need for further reform, and there is no end to it. What is essential is a revolution in man's thinking, not patchwork reform. Without a fundamental change in the mind and heart of man, reform merely puts him to sleep by helping him to be further satisfied.

*Commentaries on Living (Third Series) p.12*

# Reincarnation

329

Thought may continue, it may take another shape and form, which is called reincarnation; but does that which continues ever know the immeasurable, the timeless?

*Talks by Krishnamurti in Europe 1956 p.12*

330

A man who merely believes in reincarnation has not understood the whole problem of death and sorrow, and when he believes in that particular theory he is trying to escape from the fact of death.

*Talks by Krishnamurti in Europe 1956 p.15-16*

331

If you really believed in reincarnation, your acts, the way you think, the way you live, your callousness and indifference to everybody would disappear, because next life you will pay, you will suffer.

*Talks by Krishnamurti in India 1965 p.117*

# Relationship

### 332

To be is to be related; there is no such thing as isolated being. Relationship is a conflict within and without; the inward conflict extended becomes world conflict. You and the world are not separate; your problem is the world's problem; you bear the world in you; without you it is not. There is no isolation and there is no object that is not related.

*Authentic Report of Sixteen Talks given in 1945 & 1946 . . . p.56*

### 333

Is not relationship a mirror in which, if we are aware, we can observe without distortion our private thoughts and motives, our inward state? In relationship the subtle process of the self, of the ego, is revealed and through choiceless awareness alone can inward insufficiency be transcended.

*Authentic Report of Sixteen Talks given in 1945 & 1946 . . . p.57*

### 334

The problem is not the world, but you in relationship with another, which creates a problem; and that problem extended becomes the world problem.

*Krishnamurti's Talks 1949-1950 (Verbatim Report) . . . Ceylon p.4*

335

All relationship is a mirror in which the mind can discover is own operations. Relationship is between oneself and other human beings, between oneself and things or property, between oneself and ideas, and between oneself and nature; and in that mirror of relationship one can see oneself as one actually is — but only if one is capable of looking without judging, without evaluating, condemning, justifying.

*Talks by Krishnamurti in Europe 1956 p.54-55*

## Religion

336

If you belong to any particular ideology, to a specialized prejudice, even if you call it religion, then you will be the cause of strife and misery.

*Authentic Report of Sixteen Talks given in 1945 & 1946 . . . p.14*

337

Religion, surely, is the uncovering of reality. Religion is not belief. Religion is not the search for truth. The search for truth is merely the fulfilment of belief. Religion is the understanding of the thinker; for what the thinker is, that he creates.

*Krishnamurti's Talks 1949-1950 (Verbatim Report) . . . India p.19*

338

Religion is really experiencing a state in which there is creation. This is not an idea, a process. It can be realized when there is freedom from self.

*Krishnamurti's Talks 1949-1950 (Verbatim Report) ... Ceylon p.14*

339

What we call religion is merely organized belief, with its dogmas, rituals, mysteries and superstitions. Each religion has its own sacred book, its mediator, its priests and its ways of threatening and holding people. Most of us have been conditioned to all this, which is considered religious education; but this conditioning sets man against man, it creates antagonism, not only among the believers, but also against those of other beliefs. Though all religions assert that they worship God and say that we must love one another, they instill fear through their doctrines of reward and punishment, and through their competitive dogmas they perpetuate suspicion and antagonism.

*Education and the Significance of Life p.37*

340

Religion is not a form of conditioning. It is a state of tranquillity in which there is reality, God; but that creative state can come into being only when there is self-knowledge and freedom.

*Education and the Significance of Life p.39*

341

Organized religion is the frozen thought of man, out of which he builds temples and churches; it has become a solace for the fearful, an opiate for those who are in sorrow. But God or truth is far beyond thought and emotional demands.

*Education and the Significance of Life p.39*

342

The religions that we follow are created by our hopes and fears, by our desire for inward security and reassurance; and with the worship of authority, whether it is that of a saviour, a master or a priest, there come submission, acceptance and imitation.

*Education and the Significance of Life p.61*

343

To find out what is true religion requires, not a mere one-day effort or one-day search and forgetfulness the next day, but constant questioning, a disturbing inquiry, so that you begin to discard everything. After all, this process of discarding is the highest form of thinking. The pursuit of positive thinking is not thinking at all, it is merely copying. But when there is inquiry without a motive, without the desire for a result, which is the negative approach — in that inquiry the mind goes beyond all traditional religions; and then, perhaps, one may find out for oneself what God is, what truth is.

*Talks by Krishnamurti in Europe 1956 p.78-79*

344

Religion is not a matter of dogma, orthodoxy and ritual; it is not organized belief. Organized belief kills love and friendliness. Religion is the feeling of sacredness, of compassion, of love.

*Commentaries on Living (Third Series) p.234-235*

# Renunciation

345

Sir, have you ever tried not doing anything, really giving up, not calculating? Then you will see that life will feed you. But renunciation with a calculation is not renunciation. Renunciation with an end in view, giving up in order to find God, is merely the search for power. It is not renunciation. To renounce, you cannot look to tomorrow.

*Krishnamurti's Talks 1949-1950 (Verbatim Report) . . . India p.15*

346

When a man renounces the world in order to achieve God, in order to find something greater, is that renunciation? If I give up this in order to find that, have I really given up anything?

*Krishnamurti's Talks 1949-1950 (Verbatim Report) . . . India p.63*

347

When I renounce this world and become a monk, or a very devout religious person, the motive is that I want to achieve something better; but that is still the process of the self, is it not? I may give up my name and just be a number in a religious order; but the motive is still there.

*Talks by Krishnamurti in Europe 1956 p.75*

## Revolution

348

We think that by having an outward revolution we can bring about a new world based on what should be. On the contrary, revolution can only be at the centre, in the psyche, and then it will produce real outward revolution; but do what you will, mere outward revolution can never bring about an internal revolution.

*Krishnamurti's Talks 1949-1950 (Verbatim Report) ... India p.53*

349

Bloody revolution can never solve our problems. Only a profound inward revolution which alters all our values can create a different environment, an intelligent social structure, and such a revolution can be brought about only by you and me. No new order will arise until we individually break down our own psychological barriers and are free.

*Education and the Significance of Life* p.52

## Sacred Books

350

Why do you want to read others' books when there is the book of yourself?

*Krishnamurti's Talks 1949-1950 (Verbatim Report) . . . India* p.26

351

The man who quotes is a thoughtless man because he is merely repeating what somebody has said. Sirs, if you had no book, no *Bhagavadgita*, no Sankara, what would you do? You would have to take the journey by yourself into the unknown, you would have to venture out alone. When you discover something what you discover is yours; then you need no book. I have not read the *Bhagavadgita* nor any of the religious, psychological, or philosophical books, but I have discovered something, and that discovery can come only in freedom, not through repetition.

*Krishnamurti's Talks 1949-1950 (Verbatim Report) . . . India p.26*

352

The major calamity of modern civilization is that we are like so many gramophone records repeating what is said in the books, whether it is the *Koran*, the *Bible*, or what you will. Surely, a mind that repeats is not really in search of understanding, for it is incapable of being uncertain; and uncertainty is essential in order to find.

*Krishnamurti's Talks 1949-1950 (Verbatim Report) . . . Ceylon p.22*

353

Sirs, I am sure that in the olden days, before books were published, before there were followers, teachers and *gurus*, there were original discoverers who had never read any book. Because there was no *Bhagavad Gita*, no *Bible*, no book of any kind, they had to find out for themselves, had they not? How did they go about it? Obviously they neither had sanctions, nor did they stupidly quote the authority of some individual. They searched out the truth for themselves, they found it in the sacred places of their own minds and hearts. Surely we also can discover the truth for ourselves in the sacred places of our minds and hearts.

*Krishnamurti's Talks 1949-1950 (Verbatim Report) . . . India p.59-60*

354

No book is sacred, I assure you; like the newspaper, it is only words printed on paper, and there is nothing sacred in either.

*Krishnamurti's Talks 1949-1950 (Verbatim Report) . . . India p.78*

## Scepticism

355

Skepticism is not cynicism or denial; it is the state of a mind that does not agree quickly, that does not accept or take things for granted. A mind that accepts is seeking, not enlightenment or wisdom, but refuge.

*Krishnamurti's Talks 1949-1950 (Verbatim Report) . . . India p.68*

## Security

356

I assure you, when there is complete nakedness, utter hopelessness, then in that moment of vital insecurity there is born the flame of supreme intelligence, the bliss of truth.

*Reports of Talks and Answers to Questions . . . New York City 1935 p.11*

357

In the vitality of insecurity, there is the eternal.

*Reports of Talks and Answers to Questions . . . New York City 1935 p.18*

358

Without understanding the problem of insecurity there is no security. If we seek security we shall not find it; the search for security brings its own destruction. There must be insecurity for the comprehension of Reality, the insecurity that is not the opposite of security. A mind that is well anchored, which feels safe in some refuge, can never understand Reality. The craving for security breeds slothfulness; it makes the mind-heart unpliable and insensitive, fearful and dull; it hinders the vulnerability to Reality. In deep insecurity is Truth realized.

*Authentic Report of Sixteen Talks given in 1945 & 1946 . . . p.48*

359

We lose in the security of things made by the mind that joy of creative Reality, the very nature of which is insecurity. A mind that is seeking security is ever in fear; it can never be joyous; it can never know creative being. The highest form of thinking-feeling is negative comprehension and its very basis is insecurity.

*Authentic Report of Sixteen Talks given in 1945 & 1946 . . . p.49*

360

A mind that is seeking gain, achievement, can never find Truth. The search for gain is for security, for refuge, and Truth is not a security, a refuge. Truth is the liberator, sweeping away all refuge and security.

*Authentic Report of Sixteen Talks given in 1945 & 1946 . . . p.104*

361

As long as we are seeking inward security, the total process of life cannot be understood.

*Education and the Significance of Life p.20*

362

The very demand for inward security prevents understanding. It is only when the mind is no longer acquisitive, no longer seeking or demanding *anything*, that it is free to find out what is true, what is God.

*Talks by Krishnamurti in Europe 1956 p.5*

363

We never question whether there *is* such a thing as inward security at all, but we are always seeking it; and the very search for inward, psychological security actually prevents outward security, does it not? Obviously that is what is happening throughout the world. In our search to be psychologically secure through nationalism, through a leader, through an ideology, physical security is destroyed.

*Talks by Krishnamurti in Europe 1956 p.8-9*

364

It is only to the man who has no sense of security of any kind, that the new is revealed, because he is not concerned about himself and his achievements.

*Talks by Krishnamurti in Europe 1956 p.87*

365

Psychological dependence on another gives a false sense of security. And if it is not a person on whom we depend, it is a belief, or an ideal, or a country, or an ideology, or the accumulation of knowledge.

*Talks by Krishnamurti in Europe 1956 p.92*

# Seeking

366

**A** great scientist has no objective in his research; if he were merely seeking a result, then he would cease to be a great scientist. So it must be with our thinking.

*Verbatim Reports of Talks and Answers ..Adyar, India 1933-34 p.19*

367

**Y**ou can find enduring freedom, truth, beauty, love, which are one and the same, only when you no longer seek them.

*Verbatim Reports of Talks and Answers ..Adyar, India 1933-34 p.57*

368

**W**hat is sought after is self-created and so is not the Real.

*Authentic Report of Sixteen Talks given in 1945 & 1946 ... p.34*

369

What is it that we are seeking? We can only seek something that we know; we cannot seek something that we do not know. We cannot search for something that we do not know exists; we can only search for something that we have had and have lost. The search is the desire for satisfaction.

*Krishnamurti's Talks 1949-1950 (Verbatim Report) . . . India p.29*

370

All that the mind can do is to know itself. It must know its own limitations — the motives, the feelings, the passions, the cruelties, the lack of love, and be aware of all its many activities. One must see all that and remain silent, not asking, not begging, not putting out a hand to receive something. If you stretch out your hand, you will remain empty-handed forever.

*Talks by Krishnamurti in Europe 1956 p.22*

371

The man who understands himself seeks nothing; his mind is limitless, undesirous, and for such a mind the immeasurable can come into being.

*Talks by Krishnamurti in Europe 1956 p.22*

372

Real revolution is inward, and it comes into being without the mind seeking it. What the mind seeks and finds, however reasonable, however rational and intelligent, is never the final answer. For the mind is put together, and what it creates is also put together; therefore it can be undone.

*Talks by Krishnamurti in Europe 1956 p.64*

373

Seeking becomes another escape from the actual fact of what you are.

*Talks by Krishnamurti in U.S.A. 1966 p.44*

374

Seeking is a static state; it is not an active state. The actual state is this terrible loneliness, emptiness, this incessant demand to be happy, to find a permanent reality. Seeking is by a mind that is frightened of itself, of what it is. A man who is alive, in the deep sense of that word, *completely* fearless, is a light to himself; he has no *need* to seek.

*Talks by Krishnamurti in U.S.A 1966 p.44*

375

A mind that is full of light does not seek. It is only the dull, confused mind that's always seeking and hoping to find. What it finds is the result of its own confusion.

*Talks by Krishnamurti in U.S.A 1966 p.86*

## Self

376

If you become fully aware of one hindrance, whether it be a *guru*, memory, or class consciousness, that awareness will uncover the creator of all hindrances, the creator of illusions, which is self-consciousness, the ego. When mind awakens intelligently to that creator, which is self-consciousness, then in that awareness the creator of illusions dissolves itself. Try it, and you will see what happens.

*Verbatim Reports of Talks and Answers . . .Adyar, India 1933-34 p.84*

## 377

Does not conflict, the struggle to become and not to become, make for a self-enclosing process? Does it not create self-consciousness? Is not the very nature of the self one of conflict and pain? When are you conscious of yourself? When there is opposition, when there is friction, when there is antagonism. In the moment of joy, self-consciousness is non-existent; when there is happiness you do not say I am happy; only when it is absent, when there is conflict, do you become self-conscious.

*Authentic Report of Sixteen Talks given in 1945 & 1946 . . . p.20*

## 378

The self is the result of conformity, of conditioning, of accumulated memory; so the self is never free to discover; it can only expand in its own conditioning and organize itself to be efficient and subtle in its assertiveness, pursuits and demands, but it can never be free. Only when the self ceases to become is there the Real.

*Authentic Report of Sixteen Talks given in 1945 & 1946 . . . p.58*

379

Only in death of the self is there life.

*Authentic Report of Sixteen Talks given in 1945 & 1946 . . . p.72*

380

The ego can choose a noble purpose and so utilize it as a means for its own expansion.

*Authentic Report of Sixteen Talks given in 1945 & 1946 . . . p.86*

381

When a machine is revolving very fast, as a fan with several blades, the separate parts are not visible but appear as one. So the self, the me, seems to be a unified entity but if its activities can be slowed down then we shall perceive that it is not a unified entity but made up of many separate and contending desires and pursuits. These separate wants and hopes, fears and joys make up the self. The self is a term to cover craving in its different forms. To understand the self there must be an awareness of craving in its multiple aspects.

*Authentic Report of Sixteen Talks given in 1945 & 1946 . . . p.99-100*

382

The self is put together, made up, and the self is *not* when the parts are dissolved. But in illusion the self separates itself from its qualities in order to protect itself, to give itself continuity, permanency. It takes refuge in its qualities through separating itself from them. The self asserts that it is this and it is that; the self, the I, modifies, changes, transforms its thoughts, its qualities, but this change only gives strength to the self, to its protective walls. But if you are aware deeply you will perceive that the thinker and his thoughts are one; the observer is the observed. To experience this actual integrated fact is extremely difficult and right meditation is the way to this integration.

*Authentic Report of Sixteen Talks given in 1945 & 1946 . . . p.114-115*

383

The self, the "me" and the "mine", is very strong in most of us; sleeping or waking, it is ever alert, always strengthening itself. But when there is an awareness of the self and a realization that all its activities, however subtle, must inevitably lead to conflict and pain, then the craving for certainty, for self-continuance comes to an end.

*Education and the Significance of Life p.60-61*

384

A true artist is beyond the vanity of the self and its ambitions.

*Education and the Significance of Life p.121*

385

The self is put together, and it is only in undoing the self that that which is not the result of influence, which has no cause, can be known.

*Commentaries on Living (First Series) p.135*

386

To know oneself is an extraordinary process, because the self is never the same from moment to moment; there are so many contradictory desires, so many compulsions, so many urges.

*Talks by Krishnamurti in Europe 1956 p.34*

### 387

You cannot forget yourself by identifying yourself with the greater, that is the community! It is not an act of dissipation of the 'me', of the self. On the contrary it is the identification of the 'me' with the greater, and therefore the battle goes on, as is so obvious in those countries where they talk a great deal about the community, about the collective. The communist is everlastingly talking about the collective, but he has identified himself with the collective. The collective then becomes the 'me' for which he is willing to struggle and go through all kinds of torture and discipline, because he has identified himself with the collective, as the religious person identifies himself with an idea which he calls God. And that identification is still the 'me'.

*Talks by Krishnamurti in India 1966 p.37*

### 388

The "me", the accumulated experience as a human being, with all the knowledge, with all the accumulated information, every form of memory, treasured, cherished, and despised, put away — all that is the center which is the "me", the ego, the person, and it is that center, the psychological center, that one is afraid of losing.

*Talks by Krishnamurti in U.S.A. 1966 p.77*

389

Sir, the "me" cannot give itself up. All that it can do is to be quiet; and it cannot be quiet without understanding the whole structure and the meaning of the "me". Either that structure and the meaning can be understood totally, immediately, or not at all; and that's the only way; there is no other way. If you say, "I will practise; I will gradually work at it till the 'me' dies", then you have fallen into a different kind of trap, which is the same "me".

*Talks by Krishnamurti in U.S.A 1966 p.79*

## Self-Knowledge

390

Right thinking comes with self-knowledge. Without understanding yourself, you have no basis for thought; without self-knowledge what you think is not true.

*Authentic Report of Sixteen Talks given in 1945 & 1946 . . . p.7*

391

If the meditator does not know himself his meditation is of little value and becomes even a hindrance to comprehension. Without self-knowledge meditation is not possible, and without meditative awareness there is no self-knowledge. If I do not understand myself, my cravings, my motives, my contradictions, how can I comprehend truth?

*Authentic Report of Sixteen Talks given in 1945 & 1946 . . . p.51*

392

Know yourself; and once you understand yourself, you can deal with the problems that confront each one of us every day. Self-knowledge brings tranquillity to the mind, and then only can truth come into being.

*Krishnamurti's Talks 1949-1950 (Verbatim Report) . . . Ceylon p.5*

393

When there is no self-knowledge, self-expression becomes self-assertion, with all its aggressive and ambitious conflicts.

*Education and the Significance of Life p.15*

### 394

The ignorant man is not the unlearned, but he who does not know himself, and the learned man is stupid when he relies on books, on knowledge and on authority to give him understanding. Understanding comes only through self-knowledge, which is awareness of one's total psychological process.

*Education and the Significance of Life p.17*

### 395

When there is self-knowledge, the power of creating illusions ceases, and only then is it possible for reality or God to be.

*Education and the Significance of Life p.46*

### 396

Self-knowledge is the beginning of wisdom. But we know so little about ourselves; we do not know the unconscious as well as the conscious parts of ourselves, the totality of our whole being.

*Talks by Krishnamurti in Europe 1956 p.34*

397

The instrument of search, which is my own mind, may be perverted, twisted, and it is only through self-knowledge that the mind can be straightened out.

*Talks by Krishnamurti in Europe 1956 p.36*

398

To know yourself you need not go to any book, to any priest, to any psychologist. The whole treasure is within yourself.

*Talks by Krishnamurti in Europe 1956 p.56*

## Sensitivity

399

How insensitive we are, how lacking in swift and adequate response, how little free to observe! Without sensitivity, how can there be pliability and a quickening perception; how can there be receptivity, an understanding free of striving? The very striving prevents understanding. Understanding comes with high sensitivity, but sensitivity is not a thing to be cultivated. That which is cultivated is a pose, an artificial veneer; and this coating is not sensitivity, it is a mannerism, shallow or deep according to influence. Sensitivity is not a cultural effect, the result of influence; it is a state of being vulnerable, open.

*Commentaries on Living (First Series) p.181*

# Sex

## 400

Freedom from sex and ambition has no meaning without love. Chastity is not the product of the intellect; if the mind plans and plots to be chaste, it is no longer chaste. Love alone is chaste. Without love, the mere freedom from lust is barren and so the cause of endless strife and sorrow.

*Authentic Report of Sixteen Talks given in 1945 & 1946 . . . p.23*

401

Sex becomes a problem when we have no other release intellectually, emotionally; or rather, when there is no sensitivity, when there is no feeling — not emotion, not sentiment, not the remembrance of a past incident, of a past sensation. That is, sex becomes a problem when your being has no release except in one direction. Intellectually you have no release, because you accept, you follow; to you, the ideas are of tremendous importance, not the act, not the activity. The ideas become tremendously important intellectually, and so you have no intellectual freedom at all. Please follow all this. Intellectually you are not creative. Intellectually you are bound by authority; you are a slave to society, to respectability; you conform, and therefore there is no release through the activity of the mind. And there is no release through beauty which is sensitivity — the beauty of a tree, of the sunset, the bird, the light, the sound. You never look at a tree, never look at the sky with stars. You may go to a concert and listen to music; but again it becomes an event, but you do not live with beauty, beauty being sensitivity — sensitivity to beauty, to squalor, to dirt, to everything. Your daily activities are a boredom. Going to office, being insulted, the poverty of the mind and the heart, the utter insensitivity to life — through all that, you have no release at all. So, what happens? You have only one release: sex. And, because you have only one release, that becomes a problem.

*Talks by Krishnamurti in India 1965 p.14*

402

When there is no love in your heart, you have only one thing left, which is pleasure; and that pleasure is sex and therefore it becomes a mountainous problem.

*Talks by Krishnamurti in India 1966 p.119*

## Silence

403

Silence of the mind is not achieved by action, it is not a thing to be gone after: it comes only when conflict ceases.

*Krishnamurti's Talks 1949-1950 (Verbatim Report) ... Ceylon p.27*

404

Between two thoughts there is a period of silence which is not related to the thought process. If you observe you will see that that period of silence, that interval, is not of time; and the discovery of that interval, the full experiencing of that interval, liberates you from conditioning — or rather, it does not liberate 'you', but there is liberation from conditioning.

*Krishnamurti's Talks 1949-1950 (Verbatim Report) ... India p.74*

405

If the beginning is silence, the end is also silence. There are no means to silence; silence is when noise is not. Noise does not come to an end through the further noise of effort, of discipline, of austerities, of will. See the truth of this, and there is silence.

*Commentaries on Living (First Series) p.213*

406

There can be no silence as long as there is a seeker.

*Commentaries on Living (Second Series) p.197*

407

Silence is a state totally outside the machinery of the mind; the mind cannot conceive of it, and the mind's attempts to reach silence are still part of noise. Silence is in no way related to noise. Noise must totally cease for silence to be.

*Commentaries on Living (Third Series) p.142*

408

A man who would find a new life, a new way of living, must enquire, must capture this extraordinary quality of silence. And there can be silence only when there is death to the past, without argument, without motive, without saying, "I will get a reward."

*Talks by Krishnamurti in India 1966 p.35*

409

Quiet, stillness, silence is not a product of thought. Silence is outside the field of consciousness.

*Talks by Krishnamurti in India 1966 p.73*

410

To discover anything you must look; and to look, your look must be silent.

*Talks by Krishnamurti in India 1966 p.108*

# Simplicity

411

There can be simplicity only when the self with its accumulation ceases. It is comparatively easy to renounce family, property, fame, things of the world; that is only a beginning; but it is extremely difficult to put away all knowledge, all conditioned memory.

*Authentic Report of Sixteen Talks given in 1945 & 1946 . . . p.107*

412

Only when the mind is simple and vulnerable is it possible to see things clearly, in their true proportion. So simplicity of the mind is essential for simplicity of life. The monastery is not the solution. Simplicity comes when the mind is not attached, when the mind is not acquiring, when the mind accepts what *is*.

*Krishnamurti's Talks 1949-1950 (Verbatim Report) . . . Ceylon p.30*

413

There cannot be simplicity as long as one belongs to any particular religion, to any particular class or society, to any dogma, either of the left or of the right. To be simple inwardly, to be clear, to be vulnerable, is to be like a flame without smoke; and therefore you cannot be simple without love.

*Krishnamurti's Talks 1949-1950 (Verbatim Report) ... Ceylon p.30*

414

The man of knowledge, the man of opinion, the man of experience, will never find truth; for the mind must be very simple to find truth, and simplicity is not achieved through learning.

*Krishnamurti's Talks 1949-1950 (Verbatim Report) ... India p.49*

415

From innumerable complexities we must grow to simplicity; we must become simple in our inward life and in our outward needs.

*Education and the Significance of Life p.45*

# Social Change

416

He who is eager to reform the world must first understand himself for he is the world.

*Authentic Report of Sixteen Talks given in 1945 & 1946 . . . p.49*

417

We cannot change society; only the individual can change.

*Talks by Krishnamurti in Europe 1956 p.7*

418

Only the individual who is not caught in society, can fundamentally affect society.

*Talks by Krishnamurti in Europe 1956 p.15*

419

The social pattern is set up by man; it is not independent of man, though it has a life of its own, and man is not independent of it; they are interrelated. Change within the pattern is no change at all; it is mere modification, reformation. Only by breaking away from the social pattern without building another can you 'help' society. As long as you belong to society, you are only helping it to deteriorate. All societies, including the most marvellously utopian, have within them the seeds of their own corruption. To change society, you must break away from it. You must cease to be what society is: acquisitive, ambitious, envious, power-seeking, and so on.

*Commentaries on Living (Third Series) p.82*

420

The very structure of society is the structure of yourself. So when you begin to understand yourself, you are then beginning to understand the society in which you live. It is not opposed to society. So a religious man is concerned with the discovery of a new way of life, of living in this world, and bringing about a transformation in the society in which he lives, because by transforming himself, he transforms society.

*Talks by Krishnamurti in India 1965 p.50*

421

Society and the human being are not two different entities; when there is order in the human being, there will be order externally. Because there is disorder in all of us, there is disorder outwardly. And the mere patching up of order outside, social order — and there must be social order — will not solve this inward disorder.

*Talks by Krishnamurti in India 1966 p.28*

422

It is only in that silence, which is *very* active, that you will see, if you have gone that far, that there is a total revolution in the psyche. Only such a mind can create a new society. There must be a new society, a new community, of people who, though living in the world, are not of the world. The responsibility for such a community to come into being is yours.

*Talks by Krishnamurti in U.S.A 1966 p.39-40*

SOUL *See* **Atman (Soul)**
STILLNESS *See* **Tranquillity**

# Success

423

As long as success is our goal we cannot be rid of fear, for the desire to succeed inevitably breeds the fear of failure. That is why the young should not be taught to worship success. Most people seek success in one form or another, whether on the tennis court, in the business world, or in politics. We all want to be on top, and this desire creates constant conflict within ourselves and with our neighbours; it leads to competition, envy, animosity and finally to war.

*Education and the Significance of Life p.43*

# Suffering

424

So long as I do not know myself, the ways and compulsions of my own mind, unconscious as well as conscious, there must be suffering. After all, we suffer because of ignorance — ignorance in the sense of not knowing oneself.

*Talks by Krishnamurti in Europe 1956 p.103*

THINKER *See* **Thought and Thinker**

# Thought

425

As long as thought is anchored in belief, in ideology, it can only function within its own limitation; it can only feel-act within the boundaries of its own prejudices; it can only experience according to its own memories which give continuity to the self and its bondage.

*Authentic Report of Sixteen Talks given in 1945 & 1946 . . .p.64*

426

The created cannot think about the Uncreated. It can think only about its own projection which is not the Real. Can thought which is the result of time, of influence, of imitation, think about that which is not measurable?

*Authentic Report of Sixteen Talks given in 1945 & 1946 . . . p.108*

427

If thought is able to think about Truth then it will not be Truth. Truth is a state of being in which the so-called activity of thought has ceased. Thinking, as we know it, is the result of the self-expansive process of time, of the past; it is the result of the movement of the known to the known. Thought which is the outcome of a cause can never formulate the Causeless. It can only think about the known for it is the product of the known.

*Authentic Report of Sixteen Talks given in 1945 & 1946 . . . p.113*

428

A consistent thinker is a thoughtless person, because he conforms to a pattern; he repeats phrases and thinks in a groove.

*Education and the Significance of Life p.14*

429

Thought cannot be free nor can it ever make itself free. Thought is the result of experience, and experience is always conditioning.

*Commentaries on Living (First Series) p.180*

430

Thought cannot solve any human problem, for thought itself is the problem.

*Commentaries on Living (First Series) p.233*

431

There is no freedom of thought, because all thought is conditioned.

*Talks by Krishnamurti in Europe 1956 p.101*

432

There is no unlimited thinking, thinking is always limited; and to find out what lies beyond thought, thought must first come to an end. After all, being limited, prejudiced, shaped by society, how can thought inquire into something which is measureless?

*Talks by Krishnamurti in Europe 1956 p.111*

433

It is only when you totally deny the past which is thought, when you totally deny it every day of your life so that there is never a moment of accumulation — it is only then that you will find out for yourself a dimension which is bliss, which is not of time, which is something that lies beyond human thought.

*Talks by Krishnamurti in India 1966 p.80*

# Thought and Thinker

434

Within the pattern of duality there is no lasting answer. Each opposite has an element of its own opposite and so there can never be a permanent answer within the conflict of the opposites. There is a permanent, unique answer only outside of the pattern.

*Authentic Report of Sixteen Talks given in 1945 & 1946 . . . p.13*

435

To find the lasting solution to the conflict of duality and to the pain involved in choice, we must be intensely aware, in silent observation of the full implication of conflict. Only then will we discover that there is a state in which the conflict of duality has ceased. There can be no integration of the opposites, greed and non-greed. He who is greedy, when he attempts to become non-greedy, is still greedy. Must he not abandon both greed and non-greed to be above and beyond the influence of both?

*Authentic Report of Sixteen Talks given in 1945 & 1946 . . . p.13*

436

Are not the thinker and his thought an inseparable phenomenon? Why do we separate the thought from the thinker? Is it not one of the cunning tricks of the mind so that the thinker can change his garb according to circumstances, yet remain the same? Outwardly there is the appearance of change but inwardly the thinker continues to be as he is. The craving for continuity, for permanency, creates this division between the thinker and his thoughts. When the thinker and his thought become inseparable then only is duality transcended. Only then is there the true religious experience. Only when the thinker ceases is there Reality. This inseparable unity of the thinker and his thought is to be experienced but not to be speculated upon. This experience is liberation; in it there is inexpressible joy.

*Authentic Report of Sixteen Talks given in 1945 & 1946 . . . p.14*

437

Why does the thinker separate himself from his thought? Is it not for his own continuity? He is ever seeking security, permanency, and as thoughts are impermanent the thinker thinks of himself as the permanent. The thinker hides behind his thoughts and without transforming himself tries to change the frame of his thought. He conceals himself behind the activity of his thoughts to safeguard himself. He is ever the observer manipulating the observed, but he is the problem and not his thoughts. It is one of the subtle ways of the thinker to be troubled about his thoughts and thereby avoid his own transformation.

*Authentic Report of Sixteen Talks given in 1945 & 1946 . . . p.62-63*

438

Though you use the words 'I think', it is only a form of communication; there is actually only a state in which thought is. And thought creates the thinker, who then communicates his thought. The thinker is merely the verbalization of the thought.

*Krishnamurti's Talks Benares – India 1949 (Verbatim Report) p.38*

## 439

Is there a thinker, a centre, without thought? If you remove thought, is there a centre? If you have no thought at all, no struggle, no urge to acquire, no effort to become something, is there a centre? Or is the centre created by thought, which feels itself to be insecure, impermanent, in a state of flux? If you observe, you will find that it is the thought-process that has created the centre, which is still within the field of thinking.

*Talks by Krishnamurti in Europe 1956 p.16*

## 440

The observer, the thinker, exists only when there is the idea to transform the thought, to suppress the thought, to change the thought, to dominate the thought, to control the thought. Only when there is the activity of doing something about the thought, is there the thinker. But when that whole activity stops, there is thinking, and not the observer thinking.

*Talks by Krishnamurti in India 1965 p.66-67*

441

As long as there is the thinker and the thought, there must be duality. As long as there is a seeker who is seeking, there must be duality. As long as there is an experiencer and the thing to be experienced, there must be duality. So duality exists when there is the observer and the observed. That is, as long as there is a centre, the censor, the observer, the thinker, the seeker, the experiencer as the centre, there must be the opposite.

*Talks by Krishnamurti in India 1966 p.72*

442

You have to end seeking. For the moment you seek, you have created the object towards which you are going. As long as there is an experiencer who wishes to experience, he has created the opposite which he is going to experience. As long as there is a censor, a judge, an entity that judges, evaluates, criticizes, condemns, justifies, there must be the opposite, and hence the conflict.

*Talks by Krishnamurti in India 1966 p.72*

# Time

443

The present is of the highest importance; the present, however tragic and painful, is the only door to Reality. The future is the continuance of the past through the present; through understanding the present is the future transformed. The present is the only time for understanding for it extends into yesterday and into tomorrow. The present is the whole of time; in the seed of the present is the past and the future; the past is the present and the future is the present. The present is the Eternal, the Timeless.

*Authentic Report of Sixteen Talks given in 1945 & 1946 . . . p.31*

444

Have you not experienced in moments of great ecstasy the cessation of time; there is no past, no future but an intense awareness, a timeless present? Having experienced such a state greed begins its activities and recreates time, recalling, reviving, looking to the future for further experience, rearranging the pattern of time to capture the Timeless. Thus greed, the becoming, holds thought-feeling in the bondage of time.

*Authentic Report of Sixteen Talks given in 1945 & 1946 . . . p.31*

445

Through time the Timeless cannot be realized.

*Authentic Report of Sixteen Talks given in 1945 & 1946 . . . p.43*

446

Let us live in time timelessly.

*Authentic Report of Sixteen Talks given in 1945 & 1946 . . . p.60*

447

The now has greater significance than the tomorrow. In the now is all time, and to understand the now is to be free of time.

*Commentaries on Living (First Series) p.11*

448

Into the brain every challenge and response as experience is being accumulated; and from that accumulation we act, we think, we feel, we function psychologically, inwardly, inside the skin, as it were, and that is time.

*Talks by Krishnamurti in U.S.A 1966 p.30*

# Tradition

449

Opinion and tradition mould our thoughts and feelings from the tenderest age. The immediate influences and impressions produce an effect which is powerful and lasting, and which shapes the whole course of our conseious and unconscious life.

*Education and the Significance of Life* p. 56

450

When we are inwardly dependent, then tradition has a great hold on us; and a mind that thinks along traditional lines cannot discover that which is new. By conforming we become mediocre imitators, cogs in a cruel social machine. It is what *we* think that matters, not what others *want* us to think. When we conform to tradition, we soon become mere copies of what we should be.

*Education and the Significance of Life* p.57

451

Tradition inevitably cripples and dulls the mind.

*Talks by Krishnamurti in Europe 1956 p.13*

## Tranquillity

452

When you keep on repeating certain words, your mind becomes very still, quiet; by taking certain postures, breathing a certain way, forcing the mind, you can obviously reduce the activity of the mind. That is, through various tricks of discipline, compulsion, conformity, the mind is made still; but when the mind is made still, is it really still?

*Krishnamurti's Talks 1949-1950 (Verbatim Report) . . . India p.64*

453

When the mind is artificially made quiet, the upper layer of the mind is able to receive intimations, not only from its own unconscious, but from the collective unconscious; and the intimations are translated according to the conditioned mind. Therefore a Hitler can say he is guided by God in what he does, and somebody else in India that God is all for something quite different. It is a very simple psychological process which you can discover for yourself if you watch your own mind in action and see how it can hypnotize itself into tranquillity. Therefore, when the mind is forced into stillness through concentration, through conformity, through any kind of discipline or self-hypnosis, it is obviously incapable of discovering reality. It can project itself and hear its own ugly voice, which we call the voice of God, but surely that is entirely different from the state of a mind that is really still.

*Krishnamurti's Talks 1949-1950 (Verbatim Report) . . . India p.64*

454

As the waters of a pond become very quiet, very peaceful, when the breezes stop, so the mind is still when it is no longer creating problems.

*Krishnamurti's Talks 1949-1950 (Verbatim Report) . . . India p.65*

455

The still mind is not a conditioned mind, it is not disciplined or trained to be still. Stillness comes only when the mind understands its own ways, which are the ways of the self.

*Education and the Significance of Life p.39*

## Transformation

456

Now, is this transformation, is this radical revolution, an ultimate thing, or is it from moment to moment? I know we would *like* it to be the ultimate thing, because it is so much easier to think in terms of far away. Ultimately we shall be transformed, ultimately we shall be happy, ultimately we shall find truth; but in the meantime, let us carry on. Surely, such a mind, thinking in terms of the future, is incapable of acting in the present; and therefore such a mind is not seeking transformation, it is merely avoiding transformation.

*Krishnamurti's Talks Benares – India 1949 (Verbatim Report) p.40*

457

Transformation is not in the future, can never be in the future. It can only be now, from moment to moment.

*Krishnamurti's Talks Benares – India 1949 (Verbatim Report) p.40*

458

When you desire to be transformed , you are still thinking in terms of becoming; and that which is becoming can never know that which is being.

*Krishnamurti's Talks Benares – India 1949 (Verbatim Report) p.40*

459

Transformation can be brought about only by the individual. Great things are performed by individuals, and you can bring about a phenomenal, radical revolution when you understand yourselves. Have you not noticed in history that it is individuals who transform, not the mass? The mass may be influenced, used; but the radical revolutions in life take place with individuals only. Wherever you live, at whatever level of society you may be placed, if you understand yourselves you will bring about transformation in your relationship with others. What is important is to put an end to sorrow; for the ending of sorrow is the beginning of revolution, and that revolution brings about transformation in the world.

*Krishnamurti's Talks 1949-1950 (Verbatim Report) ... India p.5*

460

Ideas do not transform people. What brings about transformation is freedom from ideas.

*Krishnamurti's Talks 1949-1950 (Verbatim Report) ... Ceylon p.22*

461

There is radical transformation only when we understand our own conditioning and are free of it.

*Education and the Significance of Life p. 27*

# Truth

462

Truth cannot be explained or described. It *is*. I say that there is a loveliness which cannot be put into words; if it were, it would be destroyed; it would then no longer be truth.

*Verbatim Reports of Talks and Answers .. Adyar, India 1933-34 p.9*

463

If we are earnest we will find Truth; but this earnestness cannot depend on stimulation of any kind. We must give our full and deep attention to the discovery of the truth of our problem, not for a few grudging moments but constantly.

*Authentic Report of Sixteen Talks given in 1945 & 1946 . . . p 86*

464

Till we discover Truth there is no way out of our sorrows and problems. The solution is the direct experience of Truth when the mind is still, in the tranquillity of awareness, in the openness of receptivity.

*Authentic Report of Sixteen Talks given in 1945 & 1946 . . . p.100*

465

The truth is not in the distance, truth is near; truth is under every leaf, in every smile, in every tear, in the words, in the feelings, thoughts, that one has. But it is so covered up that we have to uncover it and see. To uncover is to discover what is false; and the moment you know what is false, and when that drops away, the truth is there.

*Krishnamurti's Talks Benares - India 1949 (Verbatim Report) p.14*

466

Truth is Truth, one, alone; it has no sides, no paths; all paths do not lead to Truth. There is no path to Truth, it must come to you.

Truth can come to you only when your mind and heart are simple, clear, and there is love in your heart; not if your heart is filled with the things of the mind. When there is love in your heart, you do not talk about *organizing* for brotherhood; you do not talk about belief, you do not talk about division or the powers that create division, you need not seek reconciliation. Then you are a simple human being without a label, without a country . This means that you must strip yourself of all those things and allow Truth to come into being; and it can come only when the mind is empty, when the mind ceases to create. Then it will come without your invitation. Then it will come as swiftly as the wind and unbeknown. It comes obscurely, not when you are watching, wanting. It is there as sudden as sunlight, as pure as the night; but to receive it, the heart must be full and the mind empty. Now you have the mind full and your heart empty.

*Krishnamurti's Talks Benares – India 1949*
*(Verbatim Report) p.25*

467

You can propagate an idea, but you cannot propagate truth. I go around pointing out truth; and it is for you to recognize it or not.

*Krishnamurti's Talks 1949-1950 (Verbatim Report) ... India p.5*

468

The truth of the Buddha is not the truth which you discover today. Truth is never the same, it has no continuity; it is only from moment to moment, it cannot be remembered. There is truth only when mind is completely silent. Truth is not something to be sought after, experienced, held and worshipped.

*Krishnamurti's Talks 1949-1950 (Verbatim Report) ... India p.56*

469

That which is remembered is of time, it is a thing of the past, and truth can never be of the past or of the future; truth can only be in the present, in that state where there is no time.

*Krishnamurti's Talks 1949-1950 (Verbatim Report) ... India p.56*

470

Truth is not something in the distance, there is no path to it, there is neither your path nor my path; there is no devotional path, there is no path of knowledge or path of action, because truth has no path to it. The moment you have a path to truth, you divide it, because the path is exclusive; and what is exclusive at the very beginning, will end in exclusiveness. The man who is following a path can never know truth because he is living in exclusiveness; his means are exclusive, and the means are the end, the means are not separate from the end. If the means are exclusive, the end is also exclusive.

*Krishnamurti's Talks 1949-1950 (Verbatim Report) ... India p.99*

471

Truth is not continuous, it has no abiding place, it can be seen only from moment to moment. Truth is always new, therefore timeless. What was truth yesterday is not truth today, what is truth today is not truth tomorrow. Truth has no continuity. It is the mind which wants to make the experience which it calls truth continuous, and such a mind shall not know truth. Truth is always new; it is to see the same smile, and see that smile newly, to see the same person, and see that person anew, to see the waving palms anew, to meet life anew. Truth is not to be had through books, through devotion, or through self-immolation, but it is known when the mind is free, quiet; and that freedom, that quietness of the mind comes only when the facts of its relationships are understood. Without understanding its relationships, whatever it does only creates further problems. But when the mind is free from all its projections, there is a state of quietness in which problems cease, and then only the timeless, the eternal comes into being. Then truth is not a matter of knowledge, it is not a thing to be remembered, it is not something to be repeated, to be printed and spread abroad. Truth is that which *is*, it is nameless and so the mind cannot approach it.

*Krishnamurti's Talks 1949-1950 (Verbatim Report) ... India p.100*

472

Truth is not a thing to be attained; it is seen or it is not seen, it cannot be perceived gradually.

*Commentaries on Living (First Series) p.125*

473

Truth is always new, totally unknown and unknowable. The mind must come to it without any demand, without any knowledge, without any wish; it must be empty,completely naked. Then only truth may happen. But you cannot invite it.

*Talks by Krishnamurti in Europe 1956 p.89*

474

Truth is a strange thing; the more you pursue it, the more it will elude you. You cannot capture it by any means, however subtle and cunning; you cannot hold it in the net of your thought. Do realize this, and let everything go.

*Commentaries on Living (Third Series) p.63-64*

## 475

Truth is not something abstract, something final, but it is a living thing, it is perpetually in creation.

*Talks by Krishnamurti in India 1965 p.137*

## 476

The idea of searching for truth is utter nonsense! Because to search for something implies that you are trying to find, uncover. How can you find, with a dull and repetitive mind, something which is not to be sought after, which is something alive, moving, which is totally new? So you cannot seek it.

*Talks by Krishnamurti in India 1966 p.22*

## 477

Truth is something which is not personal, which has nothing to do with any religion, with any group, with any individual; it is not to be found in any church, in any organized religion.

*Talks by Krishnamurti in India 1966 p.115*

# Understanding

478

Just experiment with it and you will see for yourself that you have the flash of understanding, that extraordinary rapidity of insight, when the mind is very still, when thought is absent, when the mind is not burdened with its own noise.

*Krishnamurti's Talks Benares – India 1949 (Verbatim Report) p.33*

479

Understanding comes swiftly, unknowingly, when the effort is passive; only when the maker of effort is silent does the wave of understanding come.

*Krishnamurti's Talks 1949-1950 (Verbatim Report) ... India p.19*

480

Understanding is a state of comprehending totally, with all one's being, nervously, emotionally, intellectually, with feeling, with everything that one has.

*Talks by Krishnamurti in India 1965 p.21*

481

You understand only when your total being comprehends — that is when you do not look at anything fragmentarily, either intellectually or emotionally, but totally.

*Talks by Krishnamurti in India 1966 p.8*

482

Understanding can only come when there is direct perception, not a reasoned conclusion.

*Talks by Krishnamurti in U.S.A 1966 p.7*

483

We are using that word "understanding" This takes place only when the crisis is great and you have no answer to it, and therefore your mind becomes completely silent; and in that silence there is an understanding. This must have happened to all of us. When you are faced with something to which you cannot possibly find an answer, you try everything; you consult, you talk it over, you inquire, you go through all the analyses, and so on, and yet there is no answer. Suddenly, when you have put it aside, as it were, there is an understanding, there is clarity, because the mind at a certain moment has become extraordinarily quiet with regard to that problem, and it is only then that there is an understanding.

*Talks by Krishnamurti in U.S.A 1966 p.61*

484

You understand something completely when you are quiet. Out of silence there is understanding, not out of your chattering.

*Talks by Krishnamurti in India 1966 p.112*

## Verbalisation

485

The more you are interested in something, the more your intention to understand, the more simple, clear, free the mind is. Then verbalization ceases. After all, thought is word, and it is the word that interferes. It is the screen of words, which is memory, that intervenes between the challenge and the response. It is the word that is responding to the challenge, which we call intellection.

*Krishnamurti's Talks Benares – India 1949 (Verbatim Report) p.33*

486

The thought is the word. Without verbalization, without the word, thought — the thought that we know — is not. So, if you see that the word — the verbalization — *is* the thought process, then it is not a question of controlling thought, but of the cessation of thinking as verbalization.

*Krishnamurti's Talks Benares – India 1949 (Verbatim Report) p.38*

487

Why do we put our responses, our reactions, into words? Why do we do that? For one obvious reason: to communicate, to tell another our feeling. Also, we verbalize in order to strengthen that feeling, don't we?, in order to fix it, in order to look at it, in order to recapture that feeling which is gone. The word has taken the place of the feeling which has gone. So the *word* becomes all-important, and not the feeling, not the response, not the experience. The word has taken the place of experiencing. So, the word becomes the thought, which prevents experiencing.

Our problem, then, is this: is it possible not to verbalize, not to name, not to give a term? Obviously it is possible. You do this often, only unconsciously. When you are faced with a crisis, with a sudden challenge, there is no verbalization. You meet if fully.

*Krishnamurti's Talks Benares – India 1949 (Verbatim Report) p.38*

# Violence

488

When your security is threatened, when your country, when your ideas, when your concept of what God is, what truth is, what should be, or what should not be, when that conceptual attitude is threatened—which makes you feel so completely insecure — then you become aggressive, violent.

*Talks by Krishnamurti in India 1965 p.98*

489

Violence is not merely physical violence, but the whole structure of the psyche is based on violence. This constant effort, this constant adjustment to a pattern, the constant pursuit of pleasure and therefore the avoidance of anything which gives pain, discarding the capacity to look, to observe *what is* — all these are part of violence. Aggression, competition, the constant comparison between *what is* and *what should be*, imitation — all are surely forms of violence.

*Talks by Krishnamurti in U.S.A 1966 p.6*

490

Non-violence is unreal to a man who is violent. The understanding of that violence is urgent, immediate, and the action of a mind that is pursuing non-violence and yet is violent, is merely sowing violence all the time.

*Talks by Krishnamurti in U.S.A 1966 p.59*

491

Man is violent and the ideal of non-violence is only an immature approach to violence. What is important is to face the violence, understand it and go beyond it, and not invent an escape, an ideal called non-violence which has no reality whatsoever, which is being shown in this country and elsewhere.

*Talks by Krishnamurti in India 1966 p.90*

# Virtue

492

We must be aware of the cunning and devious ways of the self, and in understanding them virtue comes into being, but virtue is not an end in itself. Self-interest cannot cultivate virtue, it can only perpetuate itself under the mask of virtue; under the cover of virtue there is still the activity of the self.

*Authentic Report of Sixteen Talks given in 1945 & 1946 . . . p.95*

493

Virtue is freedom, orderliness; without order, freedom, there can be no experiencing of the Real. In virtue there is freedom, not in the becoming virtuous.

*Authentic Report of Sixteen Talks given in 1945 & 1946 . . . p.113*

494

Virtue is not the denial of vice, it is a state of being, and being is not an idea. The man who cultivates virtue is not virtuous.

*Krishnamurti's Talks Benares – India 1949 (Verbatim Report) p.19*

# Visions

### 495

You want to have visions; and if you take some kind of drug, or are sufficiently conditioned in a certain religion, you *will* have visions. The man who is everlastingly thinking about Christ, or Buddha, or what not, will sooner or later have experiences, visions; but that is not truth, it has nothing whatever to do with reality. Those are all self-projections; they are the result of your demand for experience. Your own conditioning is projecting what you want to see.

*Talks by Krishnamurti in Europe 1956 p.88-89*

### 496

Our visions are the outcome of our conditioning, the religious as well as the non-religious.

*Commentaries on Living (Third Series) p.182*

# War

497

War is one of the greatest catastrophes; the greatest evil is to kill another. Once you admit such an evil into your heart then you let loose countless minor disasters. You do not condemn war itself but him who is cruel in war.

You are responsible for war; you have brought it about by your everyday action of greed, ill-will, passion. Each one of us has built up this competitive, ruthless civilization, in which man is against man. You want to root out the causes of war, of barbarity in others, while you yourself indulge in them. This leads to hypocrisy and to further wars.

*Authentic Report of Sixteen Talks given in 1945 & 1946 . . . p.10*

498

You may not be able to avert the Third World War but you can free your heart and mind from violence and from those causes that bring about enmity and prevent love. Then in this dark world there will be some who are pure of heart and mind, and from them perhaps the seed of a true culture might come into being.

*Authentic Report of Sixteen Talks given in 1945 & 1946 . . . p.15*

499

War is the spectacular and bloody projection of our everyday living. We precipitate war out of our daily lives; and without a transformation in ourselves, there are bound to be national and racial antagonisms, the childish quarrelling over ideologies, the multiplication of soldiers, the saluting of flags, and all the many brutalities that go to create organized murder.

*Education and the Significance of Life p.77*

500

There have been religious wars which have been called righteous wars. How can any war be righteous? To kill another — how can it be righteous? And our daily life of hate, competition, antagonism, ambition, seeking power, position, prestige — these bring about war. And war which is violence is the very essence of disorder.

*Talks by Krishnamurti in India 1965 p.97*

501

Wars are inevitable as long as man is living within the frontiers of an ideology.

*Talks by Krishnamurti in India 1966 p.7*

502

War is the ultimate expression of the inner conflict. There is war going on all the time, in the business world, in the political world, in the world of the religious people, between the various *gurus*, the various sects, the various dogmas.

*Talks by Krishnamurti in India 1966 p.15*

## Will

503

It is truth alone that frees, not the activity of will.

*Authentic Report of Sixteen Talks given in 1945 & 1946 . . . p.115*

## 504

What is will? Surely will is, in itself, a way of conditioning the mind, is it not? In the action of will, one dominant desire is imposing itself upon other desires, one wish is over-riding other motives and urges. This process obviously creates inward opposition, and hence there is ever conflict. So will cannot help us to free the mind.

*Talks by Krishnamurti in Europe 1956 p.28*

## 505

Silence of the mind cannot be brought about through the action of will. There is silence when will ceases.

*Commentaries on Living (Second Series) p.167*

# Wisdom

506

No Master, no teacher, no *guru*, no system, no self-discipline will ever lift for you the veil which conceals wisdom. Wisdom is the understanding of enduring values and the living of those values. No one can lead you to wisdom.

*Verbatim Reports of Talks and Answers ...Adyar, India 1933-34 p.35*

507

Wisdom cannot be bought; it is natural, spontaneous, free. It is not merchandise that you can buy from your *guru*, teacher, at the price of discipline. Wisdom, I say, has nothing to do with knowledge.

*Verbatim Reports of Talks and Answers ...Adyar, India 1933-34 p.54*

508

Wisdom is not accumulated memory but is supreme vulnerability to the Real.

*Authentic Report of Sixteen Talks given in 1945 & 1946 ... p.75*

509

The man who knows is not wise, and the man who does not know is wise.

*Krishnamurti's Talks 1949-1950 (Verbatim Report) ... India p.35*

510

Only when there is a cessation of thinking is there wisdom; and there can be cessation of thinking only when there is an end to the process of accumulation — which is the recognition of the 'me' and the 'mine'. While the mind functions within the field of the 'me' and the 'mine', which is merely reaction, there cannot be wisdom. Wisdom is a state of spontaneity which has no centre, which has no accumulating entity.

*Krishnamurti's Talks 1949-1950 (Verbatim Report) ... India p.91*

WORDS *See* **Verbalisation**

# Yoga

## 511

Yogic exercises are all right, probably, for the body. Any kind of exercise — walking, jumping, climbing mountains, swimming, or whatever you do — is on the same level. But to suppose that certain exercises will lead you to salvation, to understanding, to God, truth, wisdom — this I think is sheer nonsense, even though all the yogis in India say otherwise. If once you see that anything that you practise, that you accept, that you develop, always has behind it the element of greed — wanting to get something, wanting to reach something, wanting to break a record — , then you will leave it alone. A mind that is merely concerned with the 'how', with doing yogic exercises, this or that, will only develop a sense of achievement through time, and such a mind can never comprehend that which is timeless.

After all, you practise yogic exercises in the hope of reaching something, gaining something; you hope to achieve happiness, bliss, or whatever is offered. Do you think bliss is so easily realized? Do you think it is something to be gained by doing certain exercises, or developing concentration? Must not the mind be altogether free of this self-centred activity? Surely a man who practises yoga in order to reach enlightenment, is concerned about himself, about his own growth; he is full of his own importance.

*Talks by Krishnamurti in Europe 1956 p.88*

# You are the World

512

Can we not live without greed among the greedy, content with little? Among the unhealthy can we not live in health? The world is not apart from us, we are the world; we have made it what it is. It has acquired its worldliness because of us and to leave it we must put away from us worldliness. Then only can we live with the world and not be of it.

*Authentic Report of Sixteen Talks given in 1945 & 1946 . . . p.23*

513

You are the world, the neighbour, the friend, the so-called enemy. If you would understand you must first understand yourself, for in you is the root of all understanding. In you is the beginning and the end.

*Authentic Report of Sixteen Talks given in 1945 & 1946 . . . p.26*

514

Society is the outward expression of man. The conflict between himself and society is the conflict within himself. This conflict, within and without, will ever exist until the highest intelligence is awakened.

*Commentaries on Living (First Series) p.51*

# Appendix

## SOURCES OF QUOTATIONS

Verbatim Reports of Talks and Answers to Questions by Krishnamurti Adyar, India-1933-34

Reports of Talks and Answers to Questions by Krishnamurti New York City-1935

Authentic Report of Sixteen Talks given in 1945 & 1946 by Krishnamurti Oak Grove, Ojai

Krishnamurti's Talks Benares — India 1949 (Verbatim Report)

Krishnamurti's Talks 1949-1950 (Verbatim Report) India

Krishnamurti's Talks 1949-1950 (Verbatim Report) Ceylon

Education and the Significance of Life 1953

Talks by Krishnamurti in Europe 1956 (Verbatim Report)

Commentaries on Living (First series) 1956
Commentaries on Living (Second series) 1959
Commentaries on Living (Third series) 1961

Talks by Krishnamurti in India 1965 (Authentic Report)

Talks by Krishnamurti in India 1966 (Authentic Report)

Talks by Krishnamurti in U.S.A 1966 (Authentic Report)